SPEAK!

DALE CARNEGIE
& ASSOCIATES

SPEAK!

How to Get Over the Fear and Horror of Public Speaking

MEDIA

Published 2021 by Gildan Media LLC
aka G&D Media
www.GandDmedia.com

FIRST EDITION 2021

Interior design by Meghan Day Healey of Story Horse, LLC

Library of Congress Cataloging-in-Publication Data is available upon request

ISBN: 978-1-7225-0559-2

10   9   8   7   6   5   4   3   2   1

We all have possibilities we don't know about. We can do things we don't even dream we can do. It's only when necessity faces us that we rise to the occasion and actually do the things that until now have seemed impossible.

—DALE CARNEGIE

We would like to acknowledge the following members of the Dale Carnegie team who contributed to this book:

- Joe Hart, *President & CEO*
- Ercell Charles, *VP of Customer Transformation*
- Clark Merrill, *Carnegie Master Trainer*
- Christine Buscarino, *Chief Marketing Officer*
- Mariah Suddarth, *Trainer & Marketing Manager*
- Paul Siregar, *Managing Director for Dale Carnegie Indonesia*
- Robert Korp, *Director of Training Quality*
- Andreas Iffland, *Carnegie Master, Germany*
- Brenda Wells, *Dale Carnegie of Orange County, California*
- Rebecca Collier, *Global Master Trainer, Dale Carnegie*
- Nancy Covert, *President of Dale Carnegie Training of Birmingham and Huntsville, Alabama*
- Tina Graziotto, *Vice President of Program Management and Instruction at Dale Carnegie Training of Western and Central Pennsylvania*
- Dave Wright, *CEO of Dale Carnegie Training Houston, Austin, and San Antonio*
- Ken Beyersdorf, *President, Dale Carnegie of Arizona*
- Frank Starkey, *Vice President of Training and Master Trainer at Dale Carnegie Training of Dallas and Fort Worth*
- Berit Friman, *CEO of Dale Carnegie, Sweden*
- Mark Fitzmaurice, *Director and Master Trainer, Dale Carnegie UK*
- Jonathan Vehar, *(former) VP of Product*

CONTENTS

Part One

Structure

Part Two

Content

Part Three

Delivery

FOREWORD

by Joe Hart, CEO of Dale Carnegie Training

In May of 2015, I became CEO of Dale Carnegie Training, an organization with more than one hundred years of helping people around the world become better speakers, presenters, and leaders. Shortly thereafter, I found myself on a stage in Chicago, standing in front of two hundred Dale Carnegie leaders, where I was introducing myself and my vision for the company. While I had spoken to large groups many times in my career, and felt I was a good speaker, I was nervous. These were some of the very best trainers, coaches, and speakers in the world and I felt the pressure of presenting before such incredibly talented speakers who were watching me. Evaluating me. Judging me on my ability to present and to lead.

What gave me confidence that day were the words of Dale Carnegie, the company founder and author of the best-selling *How to Win Friends and Influence People, The*

Quick and Easy Way to Public Speaking, and *How to Stop Worrying and Start Living*. Mr. Carnegie said:

> "Sincerity and enthusiasm and high earnestness will help you. . . . When a person is under the influence of their feelings, their real self comes to the surface. The bars are down. The heat of their emotions has burned all barriers away. They act spontaneously. They talk spontaneously. They are natural.
>
> So, in the end, even this matter of delivery comes back to the thing which has already been emphasized repeatedly in [this book]: namely, *put your heart into your talks.*"

Without question, my heart was all-in that talk and with this organization. I had experienced first-hand the power of the organization's work 20 years earlier. The Dale Carnegie Course had changed my life. I walked into the course as a young attorney and came out a transformed person. People who knew me asked, "What happened to you, Joe? You seem more interested in others. You're more thoughtful—and you're more confident!" It wasn't an act. I gained a level of empathy I had lacked. And I really was more confident—so much so that I changed my career, started my own business, and eventually ended up as the CEO of this organization which has transformed countless millions of lives around the world.

When I meet with Dale Carnegie graduates, they tell me about how they had huge gains in their confidence. They found the power to unleash their enthusiasm, and to bring their heart to their work, their lives, and their families. These stories are powerful testimonials of the value of what is presented in this book. As Clark Merrill, Dale Carnegie Master, says, "Public speaking is not a trick. It's not acting . . . the key is to be yourself." My colleague Ercell Charles, VP of Customer Transformation explains its power this way: "By being yourself, you leave every audience with a unique gift, and that gift is you."

In 2015 when I walked up to that stage in Chicago for the first time to speak to the members of the organization whom I now serve as CEO, there was no doubt about my ability to be myself, to share my passion for our work, to demonstrate my enthusiasm for our new vision, and to "*put my heart into the talk.*"

An introduction to one of Mr. Carnegie's works (reprinted in the appendix) notes, "What does it take to be a great communicator? Being a subject matter expert alone doesn't guarantee a riveting presentation. Deep content knowledge may earn you the right to speak but conveying the excitement you have for your message is equally important—if not more so. If an audience senses your genuine passion for your topic, they will hang on every word. While they may appreciate your knowledge, it's your enthusiasm that will truly engage people."

The principles in this book, when applied, will help you realize that more than any tricks or tips that you might attempt when speaking, the best way to deliver a powerful message is to "be a good person skilled in speaking." Focus on being you, put your heart into your talk, and you can change the world with your words.

— All in, Joe Hart, CEO

DALE CARNEGIE'S HUMAN RELATIONS PRINCIPLES

(From *How to Win Friends and Influence People*)

Become a Friendlier Person

1. Don't criticize, condemn, or complain.
2. Give honest and sincere appreciation.
3. Arouse in the other person an eager want.
4. Become genuinely interested in other people.
5. Smile.
6. Remember that a person's name is to that person the sweetest and most important sound in any language.
7. Be a good listener. Encourage others to talk about themselves.
8. Talk in terms of the other person's interests.
9. Make the other person feel important—and do it sincerely.

Win People to Your Way of Thinking

10. The only way to get the best of an argument is to avoid it.

11. Show respect for other person's opinions. Never say, "You're wrong."
12. If you are wrong, admit it quickly and emphatically.
13. Begin in a friendly way.
14. Get the other person saying "Yes, yes" immediately.
15. Let the other person do a great deal of the talking.
16. Let the other person feel that the idea is his or hers.
17. Try honestly to see things from the other person's point of view.
18. Be sympathetic to the other person's ideas and desires.
19. Appeal to the nobler motives.
20. Dramatize your ideas.
21. Throw down a challenge.

Be a Leader

22. Begin with praise and honest appreciation.
23. Call attention to people's mistakes indirectly.
24. Talk about your own mistakes before criticizing the other person.
25. Ask questions instead of giving direct orders.
26. Let the other person save face.
27. Praise the slightest improvement, and praise every improvement. Be "hearty in your approbation and lavish in your praise."
28. Give the other person a fine reputation to live up to.
29. Use encouragement. Make the fault seem easy to correct.
30. Make the other person happy about doing the thing you suggest.

INTRODUCTION

Mark Cahill sat in the outer office of an upscale office building in New York City and was waiting to be called in to give the presentation of his career. He'd been working as a sales person for this particular large, multinational company, and was a subject matter expert on a specific piece of equipment that the company was thinking of selling internationally. If the presentation went well, it would surely mean a promotion and a raise—as well as a massive career boost.

"They're ready for you, Mr. Cahill," the receptionist said as she opened the double glass doors.

As he stood up to follow her in, Mark thought he might throw up. His head got light and all he could hear were the voices of doubt in his head. "What makes you think you'll have anything interesting to say? Don't you remember that speech class you took in high school? They literally laughed at you."

"Mr. Cahill?" The woman stood at the door, looking at him expectantly.

"Well, I can't get out of it now," Mark thought as he swallowed his nerves and headed into the conference room where the executive team sat waiting for him. "Let's get this over with."

Mark is not alone in his fear of public speaking. Research shows that as much as 77% of people around the world have some level of fear when it comes to speaking in front of others. Publicspeaking is one of the most fear-evoking events on the planet. In *SPEAK!: Getting Over the Fear and Horror of Public Speaking* we'll discover that there's no need to worry, because "it's not about the speaker, it's about the message and the audience." What this means is that one doesn't need to become some "polished professional speaker," and instead can reflect their authentic true self. Rather than focusing on being a good speaker, as Dale Carnegie put it, "Be a good person, speaking."

Our impact as a speaker comes from who we are as a person. What this means is that what makes YOU a good speaker is going to be different than what makes your neighbor, your coworker, or your sister a good speaker. So we need to stop trying to mimic our favorite great speaker (we're not them, and they're not us). Instead we must be the best person that we can be. When we do that, we'll influence our audiences.

This book reflects Dale Carnegie's thinking and what is taught in his High Impact Presentation course. It is based on the timeless principles contained in his book *How to*

Win Friends and Influence People. The stories you'll read are true, and the tips we share come from those who have mastered the art of public speaking: our best trainers around the world.

Why Public Speaking?

There are many ways to change the world and to make an impact around us. Yet nothing works without the ability to influence people, and that is the role of public speaking.

When we think of "public speaking," we envision a politician or motivational speaker up on a stage in front of throngs of people in an audience. While that is one form of public speaking, it's unlikely that any of us "regular folks" will find ourselves speaking to hundreds, thousands or even tens of thousands of people. More likely, "public speaking" will take the form of a work presentation, a speech to a group we belong to, standing up in a house of worship, or even a toast at a family member's wedding, or even a one-on-one with a customer, client or boss. In each of these settings, we are addressing a group of people with a desire to impact them in some way. We might be trying to persuade the group to invest, or to present some findings or figures. Or, we might want to honor, entertain, emotionally move, or inspire the audience. Whatever the outcome, public speaking is how we impact and change the world.

And that's why it's a critical ability.

In the words of Dale Carnegie, "Overcoming fear of public speaking impacts greatly everything that we do.

Those who answer this challenge find that they are better persons because of it. They find that their victory over fear of talking before groups has taken them out of themselves into a richer and fuller life."

Ercell Charles, the global VP of Customer Transformation for Dale Carnegie & Associates tells the story of Anh, a young lawyer for one of the most prestigious law firms in Atlanta, Ga. During one of our High Impact Presentation courses, she sat quietly to herself until someone at her table would ask her a question. When we started the program, we asked each participant to stand up and introduce themselves by telling us their name, employer, position, and expectations for the program. When it was Anh's time to stand to introduce herself, you could see Anh's reluctance as she looked down at the ground. I quickly realized that Anh was not going to offer this information without me asking her these questions. When Anh responded by sharing the law firm for whom she worked, everyone paid even more attention. So when I asked her what her reason for attending this program, it was like the floodgates opened.

"Anh exploded by saying, 'My area of expertise is Child custody and advocacy. Whenever we receive these types of cases, I am the person everyone comes to for research and developing the strategy for our clients. In addition, I am the person who provides insights and recommendations regarding the best next steps to take during the trial. Unfortunately, I am not the lawyer who is delivering these cases. Once I prep the case, I turn it over to Don, and he presents these cases before the jury. Because of my fear of speaking, I never deliver my findings in our trials. Now it has impacted my career. Guess who was recently promoted to partner in our firm? Don, not me.'

"You could tell by Anh's admission, she was both frustrated and bothered that she missed tremendous opportunities because of this fear. So, I asked Anh, 'What are you willing to do differently now that you are here?' She answered, 'Believe that I can do this!'

"To become a better speaker, the person must internally see themselves differently before becoming a better speaker externally. Before every presentation, I had Anh recite this phrase three times with confidence, 'Never again will I be afraid to stand up, speak up, and be counted!' That phrase became her mantra, and it became a launching pad to her becoming the presenter and lawyer Anh always wanted to be. As a speaker, she demonstrates confidence, capability, and the wealth of her knowledge and expertise.

"Some years later, I received a thank you card from Anh. She thanked me for what she learned in the program and said the program not only changed her career projection but changed her life. The good news was that Anh became a partner with her firm. But the great news was that Anh left that organization and started her law firm specializing in child advocacy simply because she decided to stand up, speak up, and be counted."

"It's not about becoming an orator. It's about developing your confidence in your ability to communicate your message with great impact."
—CLARK MERRILL, CARNEGIE MASTER

Classic Advice Doesn't Cut It Anymore

When we think back on some of the advice given to help public speakers "get over" their fear, some of it is downright absurd. Have you heard any of these "classic" tips?

• Imagine the audience in their underwear
• Stare at a point on the wall just over the audience's heads
• Write your key phrases on the palm of your hand
• Crack a joke to break the ice
• Pace around the stage to generate energy

This is the kind of advice that used to be given to new speakers learning to get over their fear of public speaking.

There's nothing wrong, necessarily, with wearing new clothes to a talk (unless you're trying to break in new shoes). It's that these tips, and most advice we hear, is about YOU, the speaker.

At Dale Carnegie, the most consistent piece of advice we give to people learning to improve their speaking skills is completely the opposite of this. We teach, as Clark Merrill says, "It's not about you. It's about the audience." When we focus on the message the audience needs to hear, and how it will be received by the audience, the fear of speaking dissipates. We're no longer worried about what they think of us (is my tie straight, do I have lipstick on my teeth, I hate my speaking voice, am I moving my hands correctly, et cetera). Instead, we are able to turn that energy outward and connect with the audience by being our true selves.

Step Out of "Presenter Mode"

You'll hear us talk a lot in this book about bringing out your authentic personality. That's because, at its core, being a great speaker is about bringing the best version of you to the stage. Don't try and be someone else. You can fake it for a little while, but not for long.

Robert Korp, Director of Training Quality for Dale Carnegie* puts it this way. "When I was a salesperson, I lost a significant deal when I was at the start of my career. This was a huge international company and I was giving a really important sales presentation. I was completely prepared, went in, and gave the talk. I didn't get it. Why? My friend told me, 'I am sorry, but you gave a boring impression.' Of course I was boring. I thought I had to be 'professional.' I was new and had a wrong impression and didn't share the passion for what I was doing and didn't care about the audience/potential client. What happens is we start to get nervous and focus on ourselves.

"The process to become a Dale Carnegie certified trainer is really difficult. When I went through my certification as a trainer for Dale Carnegie Training, I was in front of a group and someone was giving a talk and I was supposed to coach him. I was being observed and assessed and I was focused on myself and trying to do the right thing and I wasn't listening to him and gave him feedback that was off topic. I was too focused on myself. Lesson learned.

---

* The names and locations of the Dale Carnegie trainers and experts have not been changed.

"Now I am a certified Master Trainer and share the idea that it's not about you, the speaker. It's about the listeners. Yes, you should know your topic, but if you don't bring it alive with your authentic personality you won't be good."

Bringing the real us to the "stage" doesn't just happen. It takes work, and that's why we've written this book. It takes learning how to craft an effective presentation for that specific audience, practicing our delivery so that it feels comfortable and natural to us, and giving ourselves permission to be who we really are. The more we practice this, the less fear we'll have. The competence gained through practice, yields confidence. And that confidence will give us more opportunities to further gain competence.

In the end, YOU are your message. For us to deliver our message, we have to walk our talk, and be our authentic selves, amplified for an audience. Let's ask ourselves, "What do I do well that'll make the audience want to see and remember the message?"

Knowing ourselves

Ercell Charles, the global Vice President of Customer Transformation for Dale Carnegie & Associates says that, "Every speaker has their own marinade." In other words, we all have our own style and substance that makes us unique. If we don't know that, we're in trouble as speakers. Some speakers are naturally funny. Some genuinely earnest. Some radiate energy, or knowledge, or credibility. Some convey authentic emotion. Some light us up, and others calm us down. There's no one right way to be a speaker. As long as you're truly you.

As part of being our true self when we're speaking, we must know our vision, desired outcomes, and beliefs. Without all three, we can't be compelling. First let's focus on what we are trying to achieve. Why do we exist in the world? What is our purpose? The more clear on this we are, the more we know why we're doing what we do.

Next focus on the desired outcomes. Not just for ourselves but for others. When we're clear on our desired outcomes and how they benefit others, this helps us speak in such a way that others are interested.

And last but not least, let's be clear on what we believe. Until we know our own beliefs, we can't influence or motivate others. As Clark Merrill, Carnegie Master reminds us, "True public speaking comes from the heart." If we don't know what's in our heart, we can't move people. It is only by knowing what we believe that we can show our passion. That is what gives people hope that there is something different and better that is possible.

Clark continues, "People love diamonds, and yet marketing has a lot to do with it. They love diamonds because they're the hardest substance on earth and they sparkle. When you turn it just a bit, you get a whole different set of colors. As presenters, we are all diamonds. We are rare and we sparkle. Unfortunately, most of us, when we present in front of a group, only show one part of who we are. That's our "presenter mode." A diamond sparkles because of how it's cut and the different facets that reflect light differently. As diamonds, we all have different facets of who we are based on our life and experiences. And depending upon the audience, we can show a different facet of who we are. And in their eyes, we sparkle. This takes courage, trust, and a willingness to connect with the audience. The presenter who has the ability to do this is an outstanding communicator whose message and messages will be remembered because of the sparkle of the presenter."

In fact, passion is one core element that every Master Trainer tells us is key to effective speaking. Mark Fitzmaurice, Director and Master Trainer, Dale Carnegie UK says, "Passion is one of the most important qualities a speaker can have. The thing that's missing in a lot of speakers is that they are missing their passion and are afraid of it because they are afraid of being seen as too aggressive. Instead, we want to be passionate with grace. Passion with kindness."

This is not to say that speaking is about us. It's not. It's about them. Until we know ourselves, we can't focus on them.

It's an away game

In sports, when we go to the other team's arena, it's an "away game." While a home game may give us the advantage in that we know where we're playing, that's not how public speaking works. We have to go to them. Not necessarily literally. We have to meet them where they are, since they won't come to us just because we're on the stage. It's important for us to determine where they are in terms of the topic, what they need, and then figure out how to bring that to them in a way that they're curious, interested, and willing to be engaged.

In his still best-selling book, *How to Win Friends and Influence People,* Dale Carnegie shared the principle of "Try honestly to see things from the other person's point of view." This is a critical principle for winning friends and influencing people, which is what public speaking is all about. How do we not make it about us? By exercising our empathy to put ourselves in the shoes of our audience to determine what they need.

This piece of advice was shared with Jonathan Vehar, the former Vice President of Product for Dale Carnegie, when he was selected to deliver the graduate commencement address at Buffalo State College. "I knew I couldn't stand up and give advice to students, parents, and faculty . . . I had no real life experience to speak of. I realized that the event was an acknowledgment of many years of hard work, requiring investment and sacrifice by everyone in the arena." Jonathan engaged the graduates in publicly thanking their classmates, families, friends, and faculty for their support to help them achieve their diplomas. "To be successful," he says, "I had to help everyone feel good about being there." It wasn't about him. It was about the audience.

Thoughts from a Master: Ercell Charles, *Vice President of Customer Transformation*

If you had one piece of advice to share with someone who wants to be a better public speaker, what would it be?

"Be yourself!"
Does it sound simple? Maybe. However, this is possibly the hardest thing for most speakers to do. I have seen too many presenters try to "put on" information and deliver it like if they were wearing a new suit for the first time. Unfortunately, that doesn't work.

Whenever great speakers engage their audience, they provide three things:
1. The content
2. The delivery
3. Themselves

That last item is what makes the difference. A great presentation is never about the information alone. Nor is it just about delivery. What makes a powerful presentation is the experience the speaker gives to an audience. By being yourself and letting people see who you really are, you leave every audience with a unique gift, and that gift is you.

About this book

Despite what we said above, to be sure, it's possible to fake it. But only for a little while, and when people see through the fakery, they'll lose interest and we'll lose credibility. In this book we don't want to fake anything. This is not a book of tricks. What we present here are some ways to access what we already have inside us, straining at the leash, ready to pull us into powerful and world-changing presentations. There's nothing less at stake than being who we truly are and who we truly can be in order to change the world. One definition of leadership is to "make the world a little bit more the way we'd like it to be." That's what powerful speaking enables.

Fundamental to creating an impact with our audiences are four competencies:

1. Vision: being future oriented. Develops an exciting picture of what could and what should be, regardless of what is, for them and their organization.
2. Communication: Advances the ability of individuals and the organization through active listening, supported with meaningful oral and written presentation information.
3. Interpersonal skills: displays a consistent ability to build solid relationships of trust and respect inside and outside of the organization.
4. Audience awareness: Sees things from multiple points of view. Is mindful of how actions impact others. Keeps up to date with issues that affect areas of responsibility.

*   *   *

Rate yourself on the four competencies above. How well do these items describe your abilities? Likely you're better in some than others. For those areas where you're strong, lean into those competencies and use them to be even more effective. For those areas where you're not as strong, think about what you might do to improve upon those areas to take your skills to the next level. Either way, as you're reading this book, be open to those things that can enhance your ability to be, as Quintillian said, "a good person skilled in speaking." Some things you read in the book you'll be attracted to right away, and other things may make you scared or nervous to try. Pay attention to those things that strike an emotional chord, and try them out in a safe environment. Especially those things that scare you or make you nervous. For that is where the possibility for growth begins.

In this book, you'll learn to:
• Focus on the audience
• Deliver ideas convincingly
• Present a confident image
• Energize an audience
• Explain difficult subjects effectively
• Win skeptics to your viewpoint
• Persuade a group to take action

High-impact presenting comes from four key things: 1) Being yourself (which we've just talked about), 2) effective formats, 3) strong content, and 4) powerful delivery.

We've organized the book into three parts. The first part will cover the structure of our presentations and how to connect with the audience. The second part will cover content and how to create trust in what we're saying. The third part of the book covers the delivery of our message and how to convey our message effectively to that particular audience. In addition, throughout the book, we've included some of our preferred practices to present developed by Dale Carnegie and his trainers over the last 100 years and drawn from his book, *The Art of Public Speaking, Public Speaking: Vols 1–4, Public Speaking and Influencing Men in Business,* and *The Quick and Easy Way to Effective Speaking.*

Thoughts from a Master: Clark Merrill, Carnegie Master/ Master Trainer

If you had one piece of advice to share with someone who wants to be a better public speaker, what would it be?

Public speaking is not a trick. It's not acting. We can teach you how to act like a public speaker and you'll be able to do it. Until you're not public speaking anymore, and then you'll look like a fraud. The key is to be yourself. True public speaking comes from the heart. Martin Luther King Jr., right before he said "I have a dream . . ." looked at the audience and asked himself, "What do these people need to hear right now?" He realized that they needed hope. He spoke from the heart, and that's what people remember.

Not every talk is going to be a Martin Luther King speech; powerful speaking is something we can do when we are talking to our daughter before an important event, or any other time we want to communicate something. We ask ourselves, "What does this person need to hear right now?" and then speak from the heart.

How do we figure that out? Think about Principle 17 of Dale Carnegie's Principles. "Try honestly to see things from the other person's point of view."

From Dale Carnegie Himself

I was asked once, on a radio program, to tell in three sentences the most important lesson I have ever learned. This is what I said: "The biggest lesson I have ever learned is the stupendous importance of what we think. If I knew what you think, I would know what you are, for your thoughts make you what you are. By changing our thoughts, we can change our lives." You have set your sights on the goal of increased confidence and more effective communication. From now on, you must think positively, not negatively, about your chances to succeed in this endeavor. You must develop a buoyant optimism about the outcome of your efforts to speak before groups. You must set the seal of determination upon every word and action that you devote toward the development of this ability.

Part One

Structure

Connect on Beliefs

There's a now-classic video that was the subject of a research experiment by Daniel Simons of the University of Illinois on "selective attention," which is about people not seeing what they're not looking for.

In the video, there were two teams of three people passing basketballs back and forth to each other. One of the teams is wearing white t-shirts, the other black t-shirts. The instructions for the video is to count the number of times the team wearing white passes the basketball to each other. The audience watches, intent on getting the right answer. Not noticed by a large percentage of those who view the video is that among the teams passing basketballs marches a person wearing a gorilla costume. Mid-way through, the gorilla stops walking, faces the camera, beats its chest, and then walks off camera. It all takes about 20 seconds. Those people that didn't see the gorilla can't believe that this actually happened. In fact, they believe everyone else is lying to them. When they see it a second time, knowing what to look for, they see the gorilla (although the author knows a man in Atlanta, Georgia, who to this day believes that forty-seven other people and the instructor lied to him about the gorilla appearing in the video the first time, despite their best assurances).

Similarly, at a creativity and problem-solving conference in Buffalo, NY, a retired army colonel was giving a presentation on strategic planning. The presenter had nice, neat orderly black and white slides and photocopied handouts that were neatly typed. About 10 minute after the presentation started, with the group sitting in straight rows, a man walked in and quietly asked a woman at the back of the room what the title of the presentation was. She replied that it was "Military Approaches to Strategic Planning." The man corrected her, and said that she must be mistaken, because the schedule said that in this room the presentation was "Exploring Creativity Through Art and Color." The woman showed the man her copy of the handout with the Military title on it. And yet the man didn't believe her. Despite the fact that there was neither color nor art in the room nor was it any part of the presentation or handouts! He believed he was in the right room (he wasn't), and despite what he'd seen, he just didn't believe the woman nor what he was seeing. Instead he believed the printed schedule.

Our beliefs are powerful. They can create alignment or blind us to a reality that everyone else sees. What we believe is essential is how we can connect with people either through our shared beliefs, or by helping people believe something new by seeing a new possibility. Part one focuses on structure, and is about helping us align and shape beliefs with our audience. Until people believe you, they will never see the vision you are trying to convey.

1: PLANNING A PRESENTATION

Mark Cahill's presentation actually began several weeks before he walked into that conference room. He knew that he needed to craft a really strong opening to his talk or else he wouldn't stand a chance. In order to do this, he needed to get very clear on three things. Who is the audience? What is the purpose of the presentation? And what is the message?

First, who is the audience? Mark was a salesperson, but the audience would consist of the most senior executives of his company and their lieutenants. For the most part, he'd only seen their names on company documents or the occasional video sent out. He'd never really met any of them personally. In light of this, Mark was going to have to do a little research. What was the level of knowledge, expertise, experience, and bias when it came to the new line of business he was proposing with this specific piece of equipment? What did they want and need from the interaction? What were their goals? Was he just there to inform, or was he there to persuade them to expand the use of his equipment internationally? Was he going to need to convince them that the equipment was vital to the company in some way? And, while he did hope to "entertain" them, that surely wasn't the purpose of his talk.

Weeks earlier, as Mark powered up his computer to start to plan his presentation, he had more questions than answers. By taking the time to think it through before writing the first word, he would increase the likelihood of making the impact he wanted.

The First Question

When we are first asked to give a presentation, the natural inclination is to ask, "What's the topic?" A better question would be, "Who is the audience?" The reason for this is that in order to achieve the goal of the talk—no matter the topic—we have to connect with the audience. To do this requires developing empathy. We have to care about them and get them to care about us.

What does our audience want or need? Who are they? What's their level of knowledge or expertise? If we don't know our audience, we're at a disadvantage.

Dave Wright, CEO of Dale Carnegie Training Houston, Austin, and San Antonio shares a story that illustrates how important it is to make sure our audience is familiar with the subject matter.

"Last week I was coaching a division president for a large chemical manufacturing company. This is a multinational company. The president was giving a presentation to other senior executives and the founder of a new division they'd just acquired. The new organization's culture was very traditional and structured. Everyone was in suits— very formal. As I was coaching him, I told him, 'You need an opening that's going to get people's attention. Your product is different than what they've been offering. It's different than the standard in the industry, and better in every way, but no one knows about it—especially globally. That's the context. How familiar do you think that this audience is going to be with your product? Most don't know what it is or have it at home.' When he gave the presentation, he started with a question, 'When I talk about this product, how many of us have it in our home? How many of us have no idea what I'm talking about? Therein lies our biggest challenge and opportunity.'"

By understanding the audience's knowledge level in advance and talking about it up front, the president was able to connect better and create mutual empathy and interest. If he'd just started presenting information about a product no one knew or understood, he'd have lost them immediately.

Research is Key

What are the questions we can ask when preparing our presentation that allow us to know our audience? Begin by addressing the following questions.

• Who is the audience?
• What is the purpose?
• What is the message?

Who Is the Audience?

It is as difficult to satisfy the unknown expectations of an audience as it is to hit an unseen target. It can be done, however it is a chancy way to seek success. Part of the preparation process is the research that gathers the key information about the audience. How does one do this research? Likely we can't use our favorite internet search engine, but we can ask people. Talk to the meeting organizer. Ask some of the people who will be in attendance. Confirm this right up to the moment we begin speaking by talking to people milling about before our presentations. Let's put on our "reporter" hat and talk to as many people as we can to determine answers about the following.

When you do this badly, the consequences can be dire. A few years ago, Clark Merrill was invited to present to a client, the Administrative Office of the US Courts. Presenting just prior to Clark was a gentleman who started his presentation with, "I am proud and honored to be presenting to the AOUSC because of the great work that you do as part of the Justice Department." The audience sighed and turned to their phones. The person who invited the speaker let out a dreadful moan, because the AOUSC has nothing to do with the justice department! The speaker immediately lost all credibility, had zero attention for his presentation, and the applause was weak at best. He had failed at doing his research.

Knowledge

An obvious question is about the knowledge level of the audience. We must ask ourselves "Is the audience better informed than I am?" This is a less serious concern because the concern itself will stimulate adequate preparation, and almost always the answer is no. This should give us confidence that we are the expert in the room. The greater problem is the danger of overestimating the knowledge level of the audience. Some of us make the assumption that just because we know it, everyone knows it. That's an assumption that can cause us to lose the audience. Remember to meet them where they are, which may require us to take several steps back to ensure everyone is at the same level. Similarly, never face an audience unprepared, and also don't fall into the trap of assuming listener ignorance and talking down to the audience. Asking questions of the organizer and some attendees can help us hit the sweet spot between over- and under-estimating what they know.

Expertise

The skill level of the audience is also important because that may determine the position on the issue that we want to take. This will shape the level of the presentation we're able to give. A presentation to undergraduate students studying biology will look different than a presentation on the same topic to pharmaceutical researchers studying cancer cells.

Experience

This consideration is not only how much experience the audience has, and also at what level and in what environment. Experience in a laboratory is significantly different from experience in the field. As we seek to understand this, it's helpful to understand that someone with twenty years of experience may also have one years experience that's been repeated twenty times.

Bias

If we can identify the biases of the audience so that we can ascertain where they are starting from and some of the pitfalls we will need to avoid. Understand how they approach the topic based on what they know. If we're talking about oil drilling rights to environmental attorneys, it's helpful to know if they work for an oil company or for an ecology-based not-for-profit. They'll have a different take on the topic.

Needs

In order to send the listeners home with a sense of satisfaction and feeling glad they were there, it is critical to address their needs. Theory is important when building evidence, but eventually we must "get the hay down out of the loft so the horses can eat it." Put yourself in the shoes of the audience. What do they need to hear? What would make it worth their time? What would make it possible for them to say, "that speaker really understands me?"

Wants

Similar to needs are the audience's wants. Wants and needs are not always the same. If we only address needs, it may be more difficult to get the audience to engage. We need to eat our vegetables, but we want dessert. The best meals have a balance of the two. Similarly, a presentation that addresses what the audience needs to hear, as well as what they want from the presentation will leave them feeling fulfilled. But unlike a meal, let's give them what they want before we give them what they need.

Goals

Determine the goals/wants of our audience and keep them in mind as we plan our presentation. These days, there are many pulls on our time and attention. People show up because they have a goal, and see the speaker as a way to achieve their goals. Let's get clear about the goals of our audience and focus on helping them achieve what is most important to them.

Knowing the audience, their needs and wants and how they might view you is critical to success. Clark Merrill tells the story about a sales leader from Australia who was promoted to lead a 300 person sales team in the US. He was nervous about being seen as a foreigner who didn't understand the culture. Through conversation, Clark discovered that the new VP loved his Harley Davison motorcycle and the New England Patriots football team. So Clark advised him to ride his Harley Davidson motorcycle up onto the stage, announcing how much he loved riding his Harley. What an entrance! The VP then threw five footballs into the audience as he told them how much he loved the New England Patriots. Keep in mind that this was completely authentic for the VP! He started off strong, and continued to share his vision for how the sales team would be successful by working together. At the closing, he asked everyone who had caught one of the footballs to stand up and reach inside a slit that was cut in the foam footballs. Inside was a neatly folded $100 bill. As jealous as they were, everyone started cheering for those who had caught the valuable footballs. The VP closed by asking the audience, "If you'd known there was $100 in the football, would you have tried harder to catch it? That $100 is nothing compared to what we'll generate as a sales team together when we all try harder." His close drew the entire audience to their feet as they gave him a standing ovation.

In this chapter, we covered the research needed to understand the audience to whom we'll be presenting. In the next one, we'll go into how to craft a powerful and engaging opening.

Thoughts from a Master: Paul Siregar, *Managing Director for Dale Carnegie Indonesia*

If you had one piece of advice to share with someone who wants to be a better public speaker, what would it be?

- Have a clear objective of what you want to achieve through your presentation. Is it just to inform, or to convince/persuade, or to inspire, or something else?
- Have a clear storyline to get the audience from where they are to where you want them to be. A storyline is the logic of the argument peppered with convincing evidence.
- Have an engaging starting point (opening) to capture the audience's attention and interest. Consider stories, questions or startling statements.
- Have a specific call to action to compel the audience to act upon our message. What's the sense of us speaking if it doesn't move the audience?

From Dale Carnegie Himself

Should you rehearse your talk after you have it in some kind of order? By all means. Here is a sure-fire method that is easy and effective. Use the ideas you have selected for your talk in everyday conversation with your friends and business associates. Instead of going over the ball scores, just lean across the luncheon table and say something like this: "You know, Joe, I had an unusual experience one day. I'd like to tell you about it." Joe will probably be happy to listen to your story. Watch him for his reactions. Listen to his response. He may have an interesting idea that may be valuable. He won't know that you are rehearsing your talk, and it really doesn't matter. But he probably will say that he enjoyed the conversation.

2: OPENING

Mark Cahill was nervous and he still had several weeks to go before his presentation. He wasn't a professional speaker and had no idea how to start a presentation. "Maybe I'll just get up there and introduce myself," he thought. "Or, I could tell a little joke?" He walked over to the full length mirror hanging on the back of his office door and practiced his opening. "Hi, I'm Mark Cahill and I'm really glad to be here today. Some weather we're having, right? That reminds me, did you hear the one about the airline pilot . . ." Shaking his head no, Mark realized that would be a disastrous way to start his talk. He remembered his dad telling him, "You only get one chance to make a first impression.

Openings Matter

How we open our presentation sets the tone for the rest of the talk. Paul Siregar, Managing Director for Dale Carnegie in Indonesia says, "Recently, the Marketing Director of Indonesian operations of a multinational oil giant recalled the time two years ago when he noticed that the members of another team started to deliver their presentations differently. The way they opened their presentations was interesting as they were using a variety of openings, such as a photo, a story, etc. He asked about it and found out that the thirty members of the team had just attended Dale Carnegie's High Impact Presentations program. He told me that's how he realized how important an opening is to a presentation, and why he changed his approach to be more effective."

There are two critical points of an airplane flight: take-off and landing. The same is true of presentations. A strong opening will create additional confidence, and an opportunity to make an immediate positive first impression.

Our goal with the opening is to immediately gain favorable attention, to lead naturally into our presentation, to build goodwill, and to create points of agreement with the audience so they know that we're on the same side.

Four Types of Openings

There are four basic types of openings and within each type there are several ways to approach it. The four types are as follows:

1. Captivating Statement
2. Question
3. Story
4. Prop/exhibit

Let's take these one at a time and look at the options and some examples of them in use.

Captivating Statement

With a captivating statement, our goal is to grab their attention immediately and get them thinking. There are three ways we can do this to open a presentation: Analogy, Startle, and Good News.

Analogy is the comparison of the similarities of two dissimilar objects or ideas. Everything else is a comparison. It should be easily understandable so that people can relate: "I remember the first time I flew on an airplane. I was scared at first because it was unfamiliar. When I relaxed and trusted the expertise of the pilot, I began to enjoy the adventure. That's how many of you are feeling now, as new employees here."

When we startle, we want to jolt people out of their complacency immediately so that they pay attention: "Look around the room. The vast majority of you won't be completing this program in four years. Most of you will take five or six."

If it's appropriate, and only if it's fitting, starting with Good News can put everyone in a positive frame of mind: "This was the best quarter our company has ever seen in terms of sales orders. This means that everyone here reached the highest commission tier possible!"

Note: This does not work when announcing layoffs, at a funeral, or anywhere else where the mood is likely to turn somber. It must be appropriate for the circumstances.

Question

Why might we want to open our talk with a question? What's your answer?

Because by doing so, we get people thinking immediately and spark their curiosity. We can use this approach to gain information, get participation, or to get agreement on a need or interest.

There are two absolute rules for opening with a question:

1. Get an answer from the audience. Repeat the question if necessary. This forces people to check in and lets them know that something different is going to happen. Especially if you're following another speaker.
2. Ask an easy question.

Gaining information helps us learn more about what our audience is thinking, and also engages them immediately in the conversation so that they're not just sitting passively: "Customer spending has decreased over the last year. What might be some of the reasons this is happening?"

Starting with a strategy to get participation is another way to engage people immediately: "Let's take a survey. Raise your hand if you've ever had a bad experience with customer service."

One of the principles from *How to Win Friends and Influence People* that is helpful in winning people to your way of thinking is to "get the other person saying, 'yes, yes' immediately." "If there were a way to lose weight, have more energy, and still eat the food you love, you'd want to know what it was, right?"

Story

Dale Carnegie recognized the power of stories. They are powerful and are how we learn. And when someone is telling a story, we are entranced, which makes them powerful when giving a presentation. Key is to make it a short story. There are three ways to open a talk that share an incident or anecdote. They are personal experience, third party, or historical.

The story should start with a time and a place, and without preamble. "It was July 2011 in Minneapolis, MN. It was a beautiful summer weekend . . ." Don't start with, "I'm going to tell you about a time when . . ." There is no need for this. Jump in.

A story told from Personal Experience is the most powerful: "The first time I got fired, my boss did it through a text message."

Less powerful is to tell the story that belongs to someone else: "When I was a child, my grandfather used to tell me about life growing up on a farm . . ."

Another effective approach is to share historical stories: "Marie Antionette is famous for saying 'Let them eat cake.' Well, she's famous for one other thing, too . . ."

Sharing an incident that links to the talk can be a powerful way to engage the audience from the start. The challenge is to ensure that the incident links to the big idea of our presentation. Think carefully about what we want the audience to take away from the incident, and then we can shape our story to reinforce the key point. Avoid distracting details that don't reinforce the point we're trying to make. Does the color of the car matter? Probably not. Unless we're telling a story about how someone changed the color of a car in order to demonstrate a new painting technique.

Prop/Exhibit

People love props. Very little brings an idea or a concept to life like an exhibit that turns an idea into reality. Some important guidelines:

1. Make sure it has something to do with what you're going to talk about. A six-foot stuffed giraffe that has nothing to do with your topic is distracting.
2. Hold it up high enough that everyone can see it, next to, not in front of, your face. Don't speak to the back of the prop. And when everyone can see your face, they can see your prop.
3. Put it down when you are done. Do not pass it around. People will want to play with the prop, and will stop listening to your message.

Use Your Own Material

Regardless of which type of opening we use, make sure to use it authentically. Otherwise it can fall flat and backfire. Frank Starkey, Vice President of Training and Master Trainer at Dale Carnegie Training in Dallas shares this personal (and embarrassing) story. "The worst class I ever took was Speech 101. We were told to open with a story.

Well, I was young and didn't have any interesting stories so I 'borrowed' one that my dad used to tell. It was about a time when he'd been working at a morgue and, long story short, the dead guy woke up. It was pretty clear that there was no way this could have happened to me, and the result was that the audience was more confused than interested." When the story and material are our own, we can be much more effective in painting the picture for the audience. We can be confident while talking about it, and can field questions that demonstrate our credibility.

More Tips For Crafting Your Opening

Dave Wright, CEO of Dale Carnegie Training Houston, Austin, and San Antonio offers these tips for crafting our openings.
- Open quickly
- Be creative and engaging
- Create context right away (in a moment). "The whole world has changed. Our business model is illegal. We are at war."
- Tell stories. Be human. It's okay to get emotional, but not fall apart.

Nancy Covert, President of Dale Carnegie Training of Birmingham and Huntsville, Alabama shares a story about how one company captured attention during a very early safety meeting. "NuCor is a huge steel company, one of our biggest customers. They have a safety meeting every morning at six am which requires someone to give a safety talk. When they have participants attending High Impact Presentations, they go to the safety meeting and then practice what we taught the day before. The challenge is that these people attending the safety meeting are ending a twelve hour shift and are tired. They don't want to sit there and listen to safety information, they want to go home. To capture their attention, I started with, 'Everyone raise your hand.' They all raised their hands. 'Now, how many of you want to go home with all of your fingers today?' That got their attention!"

These are not people who want to be public speakers. They have to give a safety talk and want to make it more engaging. By making it relatable to their specific audience, they keep the audience from tuning out the important message that may keep them safe and potentially save their lives.

In the next chapter, we'll get into what happens after we've opened the presentation and are now ready to get to the heart of the message.

Thoughts from a Master: Dave Wright, CEO of Dale Carnegie Training Houston, Austin, and San Antonio

If you had one piece of advice to share with someone who wants to be a better public speaker, what would it be?

The most difficult but powerful change for people is to shift their focus. Can we make the transition from being self-conscious to being able to really think in terms of how we are adding value to the people we are talking to, both intellectually and emotionally? Presentation skills are leadership skills because it's about influence. It's about where we want them to be at the end and how to structure the message to get the audience there.

From Dale Carnegie Himself

Speakers who talk about what life has taught them never fail to keep the attention of their listeners. I know from experience that speakers are not easily persuaded to accept this point of view—they avoid using personal experiences as too trivial and too restrictive. They would rather soar into the realms of general ideas and philosophical principles, where unfortunately the air is too rarefied for ordinary mortals to breathe. They give us editorials when we are hungry for the news. None of us is averse to listening to editorials, when they are given by a person who has earned the right to editorialize—an editor or publisher of a newspaper. The point, though, is this: Speak on what life has taught you and I will be your devoted listener.

3: MESSAGE

Mark Cahill sat in front of his computer with a bit of writer's block. After all, he was a sales guy, not a writer. He'd chosen an opening (he was going to start with a story) and felt confident that he could capture the audience's attention. What next? It's one thing to tell an engaging story. It's a completely different thing to focus the audience's attention on the subject.

The Message

Once the opening has captured the attention of the audience, it is necessary to establish the theme or message of the presentation. As in a fine symphony where the composer reveals the theme and then proceeds to create variations on it, the speaker presents the message and then proceeds to develop it with facts, information, and evidence. All while staying true to the theme of the talk.

The opening is designed to get the attention of the audience. The message statement *focuses attention on the subject.* It can be a statement of intent, such as: "We are now going to examine the pros and cons of the new hiring process." It can be a question such as: "What are the steps necessary to increase revenue ten percent by December 15 of next year?" Sometimes the message statement is presented as a proposal of logic such as, "If . . . is true, then . . . is also true, and . . . is the natural result." The message statement guides the development of the presentation and keeps it from straying away from the purpose or objective.

Tina Graziotto, Vice President of Program Management and Instruction at Dale Carnegie Training of Western and Central Pennsylvania offers this suggestion for crafting a message that gets the audience focused. "My advice is that you have to be clear about what your message is. If you're not clear then you're going to fail."

To put it another way, as Cavett Robert said about church sermons, "If it's hazy in the pulpit, it's cloudy in the pew."

What's The Point?

To do this, it's important to stay focused on one question. "What are you trying to accomplish?" In the case of Mark Cahill, he's trying to persuade the executive team to expand the use of his equipment internationally. Because it's a persuasive talk, as opposed to another type of presentation, he'll need to craft the theme of his message with the end goal of persuasion in mind. To start, he asked himself,

"How can I make a presentation about a piece of mechanical equipment interesting to people who aren't familiar with it?"

Nancy Covert, President of Dale Carnegie Training of Birmingham and Huntsville, Alabama, came upon a very similar challenge.

"A couple of summers ago, we were in Alabama, doing presentation skills training. The audience was made up of twenty line workers with the power company. They weren't exactly expert presenters. After all, you go to lineman school not presentation training. None had ever spoken in front of a group. Their whole speaking experience related to what we called, 'toolbox talks.' These talks focused on being safe, dehydration, heat stroke et cetera. Frankly, no one wants to listen to this kind of talk let alone give it.

"The talks were taken from a thirty page document from health and safety and was full of medical terms. It was awful. We took a day with the leadership team and sat down and tore it apart and made it connectible to other line workers.

"As an example, they were trying to help the line workers understand when they needed to drink more water. The answer related to their urine color. But instead of using complex medical terms, they used food coloring in bottled water to illustrate different colors of urine and then allowed the audience to examine them. They kept it fun by taking the last bottle and instead of water, they used Mountain Dew, so that when they tossed that bottle to the audience, the Mountain Dew fizzed. It was fun and memorable and engaging. After they started using this approach to their 'toolbox talks,' there were zero incidents of dehydration."

While this story may be a little off-color, it's a powerful example of how to take something boring and create something relatable and memorable to protect the health and safety of others.

Relatable and Memorable

Some subjects are difficult to communicate in a meaningful way. Ercell Charles, the global VP of Customer Transformation at Dale Carnegie & Associates worked with some of the world's experts in the field of bioterrorism to help them present more effectively. "One of the most powerful training techniques we use," he says, "is called 'coaching in the moment.' While recording the presenter, we coach the participant to add insights and opportunities to enhance their presentations based on their vision or desired outcome. One global expert stood up to give his presentation. With his manual in hand, he stood in front of the audience and read his presentation from the manual. I responded by saying, 'Stop! Great start Doctor. When connecting with people, we don't want any barriers, so let's start again without the manual.' Dr. Sterling looked over his glasses and reluctantly agreed to start over. Without the manual in hand, the doctor started again, spoke for approximately 15 seconds, then picked up the manual again and once again started reading from his notes. 'Stop! Doctor, you connected with the group from the start. Let's not lose that connection with the audience by picking up and reading from your manual. Please let's start one more time.'

"Feeling a little challenged, the doctor started his presentation yet again, and once again, after 15 seconds, he picked up his manual and read from his notes. This time, to demonstrate that it was important, I walked up and took the manual out of his hands. 'Now, that is rude!' he shouted. I apologized and allowed him to finish his report with minimal coaching.

"At the end of this presentation, we took a break, and I pulled the doctor aside to apologize for my actions. He accepted my apology and told me that he understood what we were attempting to accomplish with the coaches. During our discussion, I shared with the doctor that the audience doesn't care about how much information you have or how much you know about a subject. They can research or Google that information. What they truly care about is your experience with what you know. Your perspective based on your experiences is just as critical as the information itself. That resonated with the doctor. His following presentations were filled with anecdotes, analogies, and stories about important topics related to his field and expertise, which helped he to be much more effective in sharing critical information in a powerful and memorable way."

Nancy Covert shares another powerful story of how important it is to connect the message to the audience.

"We had a large bank in Birmingham going through our training. They cover eleven southern states (from California to Florida) and the Executive Vice President was in a national sales meeting, bored to tears.

All the Senior Leaders were just going through the motions. Afterwards, they hired us to train the bank leaders. After all, it's expensive to have these meetings, and if you don't even communicate the CEO's message effectively, you're wasting time and money.

"The next sales meeting was like night and day. We worked together and came up with a creative way to communicate the CEO's core message which was 3/3/3. He was trying to get the sales team to contact customers three days later, three weeks later, and three months later after an interaction. One of the senior executives opened his talk with a question. 'How many of you have gone out on a first date with someone and over dinner you share your hopes, dreams and financial situation and you feel connected. But then they never call you again? That doesn't feel good, does it? Similarly, we need to call our customers because they told us personal things. Three days, three weeks, three months.' He was able to make the vision and mission relatable and memorable."

The possibilities for messages are endless. Be sure to connect the message with the audience in a way that they will hear it, internalize it, and remember it. When we make it meaningful for them, we'll be well on our way to being a successful speaker.

So far, we've talked about how to research the audience, craft a compelling opening, and convey a meaningful message. In the next chapter, we'll talk about one of the most important parts of any presentation—the closing.

Thoughts from a Master: Robert Korp, *Director of Training Quality EMEA for Dale Carnegie*

If you had one piece of advice to share with someone who wants to be a better public speaker, what would it be?

Love. Love what you do, love your topic, and love your audience. There's no bad speaker. Only the wrong subject.

Remember Dale Carnegie's Three E's. 1) You have to have Earned the right to speak based on experience, knowledge, what you do, and how you have lived. 2) Excitement. Be excited about what you have to say. And 3) Eagerness to share the value.

We all know there are subjects we don't love. Even if it's a financial report, you still have to find some passion.

4: CLOSING

Mark Cahill was taking a break from creating his presentation. He had to go to a tech conference and was listening to the keynote speaker. As he sat there and listened to the speaker droning on and on in a monotone voice, he found himself looking around the room. The talk was supposed to end fifteen minutes ago, and the audience was getting restless. People were starting to check their watches or sneak peeks at their phones. Some people were even getting up and leaving!

The speaker seemed oblivious to it, too. Did he not know how to end the talk? Mark couldn't help thinking that the speaker was missing a key opportunity to bring home the points in the talk. "I need to make sure I don't do this," he thought to himself.

"When you get to the close, stop talking.
Just stop talking. End it on a high note."
Clark Merrill, Carnegie Master/Master
Trainer at Dale Carnegie & Associates

We've all been there. We're listening to a talk or presentation and it's supposed to end at a certain time, and the speaker is still going. There's no new information being presented, and the speaker is just repeating what has already been said.

Dale Carnegie says that the closing is one of the most important parts of the talk. It has to be crafted with intent and care so that we can leave the audience with a lasting final impact. Just as the opening of a presentation creates a positive first impression, the closing creates the last impression.

Clark Merrill worked with a VP of Marketing who was giving two identical presentations to each half of the employee group due to the limitations of the room capacity. The first of the two presentations started strong and went well. Twenty minutes into the talk, when he got to the close of the presentation, he kept talking. Ten minutes later, he had managed to sap all the energy from the audience, and when he finally ended, he received tepid applause. After the first presentation, when asked why he kept going, the VP said "Clark, I was in the zone!" Clark told him, "You were in the Twilight Zone, and you lost the audience. In the afternoon session, if you don't stop at the close, I'm going to come up on stage and stop you, and since everyone in the company knows me, they'll thank me." The VP took the coaching. In the second presentation, when he got to the close, he ended strongly. And promptly received a standing ovation. "When you get to the close, stop talking. Just stop talking. End it on a high note."

How can we make sure that our last impression is a good one? Here are some tips.

- Persuade with logic
- Inspire with emotion
- Be brief
- Build to a crescendo so your last words have impact
- Tie back to your opening or the theme of your message
- Speak on a personal level
- Dramatize ideas
- Use a visual that has great impact

We can see that these ideas are extensions of what we want to be doing throughout the talk. The closing should be a natural climax to the energy and momentum that we've been building all along. Here are some examples of the types of closings we can use, depending on the purpose of our talk.

Tie the opening to the close

One of the most effective ways to close is to tie the opening to the close. This brings the story full circle and gives you the opportunity to make the presentation feel well-integrated.

Recall watching a movie with an opening scene that was out of context with the true beginning of the movie.

Or reading a book with a Prologue that takes place at a later point in time as Chapter One. Then, when you get to the part of the movie or book that explains that opening scene, you think, "Oh yeah! It makes sense now!" We should strive to do this with our presentations as a way to keep our audience curious and interested to hear how the story ends. Leaving the ending unresolved keeps the audience thinking and engaged until we finally reveal what happened.

As you recall there are four types of openings in presentations. Here are some ways we can tie the closing back to the opening.

1. **Captivating Statement**: "As I said in the opening, by the time we got to the end of our time together today, 20,000 babies will have been born. Those children are here, now, and deserve a better world. Thank you."

2. **Question**: "Earlier, I asked you, 'What kind of world do we want to leave our grandchildren?' Not only do we have the answer to that question, but we have an action plan for how to get there."

3. **Story**: "You may recall the story of Mary Alice, the girl who had a little lamb with fleece as white as snow. Well, Mary is all grown up now . . ."

4. **Prop/exhibit**: "When I first showed you this device, it seemed like something out of a science fiction novel. But this technology is here and now, available to all of us."

Purpose: To Convince or Impress

Repeat major benefit

"So, make these two simple changes and you can be thriving in business, two years from now, ten years, twenty years. First . . ."

Use a quotation from an expert

"It isn't what you have, or who you are, or where you are, or what you are doing that makes you happy or unhappy. It is what you think about." —Dale Carnegie

Purpose: To Inform

Repeat your key point(s)

"Finally, remember the three most important words in real estate: location, location, location."

Recap the steps of a process or plan

"Let's remember to follow these simple steps to assure consistency and save time for everyone. Step one is . . ."

Purpose: To Persuade

Action and benefit

"Contact a customer today and ask why they like doing business with us and you will create champions who will help increase your sales."

Final Recommendation

"In conclusion, we recommend the third option discussed, which will have the greatest impact on our customers."

Purpose: To Inspire

Throw down a challenge

"Let's cross this Rubicon together. It won't be easy, but we can do this. We should do this . . . for the sake of the colleagues who will follow in our footsteps."

Appeal to nobler motives

"Let's create a greener planet for our children and grand-children."

Andreas Iffland, Carnegie Master in Germany shares an anecdote about a client who was giving a presentation and used the "Final Recommendation" close.

> "I was working with a man named Axel who told me, 'I have a very important presentation next week. I am the National Director of Sales for Germany and have twenty salespeople working for me. I want to add a layer of leadership from the outside and know they are not going to be happy about it. I want to communicate my decision effectively without losing people.'
>
> "We worked together to structure his talk so that they could see the reasons for his decision. He talked about the problem they were facing (the sales team had gotten too large for one manager) and the three

options for solving the problem. As he listed the three options, he then went through the advantages and disadvantages of each and then gave his opinion so that the group could see that he had considered all views. He did this and said it went extremely well. Afterward, they said 'We understand why you made a different choice.'"

Certainly the National Director of Sales for Germany could have told the twenty sales people what the change was, and then let them get used to it. Instead, he put himself in their place by thinking about what they needed to know and how they might want to hear his thinking. This enabled him to help them not just hear the decision, but understand why he made it. Principles 17 and 18 from Dale Carnegie's, *How to Win Friends and Influence People* advise us to "Try honestly to see things from the other person's point of view," and "Be sympathetic with the other person's ideas and desires." When we do that, we can deliver an inspiring presentation.

In this chapter, we've talked about the different ways we can close our presentations. Now that we've laid out the structure of our talk, Part Two of this book will delve into the "heart" of the matter—how we can create trust with the audience.

Thoughts from a Master: Andreas Iffland, Carnegie Master, Germany

"If you had one piece of advice to share with someone who wants to be a better public speaker, what would it be?"

My advice is simple. Be authentic. Most people misunderstand this. I want to push people out of their comfort zone. I tell them to be more animated and they say, "That's not me." But it's in everyone. Don't play a role or be an actor. When you come off as unnatural you lose credibility. Don't use "being yourself" as an excuse to do it like you did it before. Instead, be the best version of yourself.

From Dale Carnegie Himself

How do you go about bringing your talk to a climactic close? Here are a few suggestions:

SUMMARIZE. In the longer talk a speaker is very apt to cover so much ground that at the close the listeners are a little hazy about all his main points. However, few speakers realize that. They are misled into assuming that because these points are crystal clear in their own minds, they must be equally lucid to their hearers. Not at all. The speaker has been pondering over his ideas for some time. But his points are all new to the audience; they are flung at the audience like a handful of shot. Some may stick, but most are liable to roll off in confusion. The hearers are liable, in the words of Shakespeare, to "remember a mass of things but nothing distinctly." Some anonymous Irish politician is reported to have given this recipe for making a speech: "First, tell them what you are going to tell them; then tell them; then tell them what you have told them." It is often highly advisable to "tell them what you have told them."

ASK FOR ACTION. In your final words of a talk to secure action the time has come to ask for the order. So ask for it! Tell your audience to join, contribute, vote, write, telephone, buy, boycott, enlist, investigate, acquit, or whatever it is you want them to do. Be sure to obey these caution signs, however: Ask them to do something specific. Don't say, "Help the Red Cross." That's too general. Say, instead, "Send your enrollment fee of one dollar tonight to the American Red Cross, 125 Smith Street in this city." Ask the audience for some response that is within their power to give. Don't say, "Let us cast our ballot against the Demon Rum." It can't be done. At the moment, we aren't balloting on the Demon Rum. You could, instead, ask them to join a temperance society or to contribute to some organization which is fighting for prohibition. Make it as easy as you can for your audience to act on your appeal. Don't say, "Write your congressman to vote against this bill." Ninety-nine percent of your listeners won't do it. They are not vitally interested; or it is too much trouble; or they will forget. So make it easy and pleasant to act. How? By writing a letter yourself to your congressman, saying, "We, the undersigned, urge you to vote against Bill No. 74321." Pass the letter around with a fountain pen, and you will probably get a lot of signers—and perhaps lose your fountain pen.

Part Two

Content

The Trust Formula

When we're speaking to an audience, whether it's large or small, we're trying to create trust in the room—trust in what we're saying, trust in the audience, trust in the speaker. In order to create trust, we need to demonstrate credibility and empathy.

$$Trust = Credibility + Empathy$$

Credibility is about getting the audience to believe us. It's about earning the right to speak to them, and then defeating any doubts they might have. They must believe in us and our ability to lead them through the presentation, otherwise they won't be willing to be engaged or have their thinking shaped by what we have to say. We can't do that by being something or someone we're not.

Empathy is all about understanding our audience at a very deep level. It's about putting ourselves into their lives to determine what it is that they need to hear from us so that they're willing to take action.

5: CREDIBILITY

In order for Mark Cahill to convince and persuade his audience, he is going to need to have credibility and to be seen as an expert on the subject. In his case, he's got a good head start because he is a subject matter expert on the technology they're considering for the expansion. Having the knowledge and being a credible speaker are two different things. Mark knows that he needs to be able to demonstrate his competence in order to achieve the goals of his presentation.

Credibility Starts With Three Es

In order to establish credibility with our audience, we need to demonstrate the Three Es.

1. We must have **Earned the right** through experience or study to be able to talk about our subject and tell our stories.

2. We must be **Excited** to share, without trepidation or hesitation.

3. We must be **Eager** to share because we want to convey value to the listener.

It all comes back to being ourselves. Assuming the three E's are there for us, then we trust that we have the ability to convey credibility and are able to effectively speak on the topic.

Rebecca Collier, Global Master Trainer, Dale Carnegie shares a story about how a third generation member of a long standing family business—we'll call him Lee—earned his audience's credibility.

"In this company, which had been family owned and operated for more than eighty years and was dominant in their marketplace nationally and internationally, family members had to start at the bottom and work their way up. What that meant was that most of the people in the audience knew Lee's siblings, parents, and grandparents. The audience was made up of high level Vice Presidents and General Managers. Lee didn't have the same experience as they did, however he had the family DNA.

"When he gave his first presentation, Lee was a little shaky and you could sense how uncomfortable he was. By the final presentation, about inspiring people to make change, you could FEEL the admiration and respect Lee had earned from the senior people in the room. It was rock solid. He and his generation who will inherit the leadership have a different level of confidence. The turning point for Lee was training in being a great person speaking, which enabled him to develop his credibility not based on his name but based on who he is as a person."

That's the theme that keeps coming up again and again in the experts we talk to. Being an effective public speaker is about bringing who we are as a person to the presentation. It's a mindset and an energy, not a trick or technique. When we project to our audience that they are receiving something of value and significance, they will believe us.

Going Downhill

Ercell Charles, the global VP of Customer Transformation for Dale Carnegie & Associates was working with a group on public speaking which included a regional sales director for a construction company out of North Carolina. Ercell says, "He was impeccably dressed, engaging, and very conversational. In his group in the course, he led some of the conversations, and we noticed how well he engaged others within his group. My initial reaction while witnessing this interaction was to reach out at the break and ask him if he registered for the wrong program! So, I reached out to him during the break and asked whether he signed up for this program. Without hesitation, he said, 'Yes, this is the program I signed up for.' I asked him, 'So you are ok with remaining in this class?' He said, 'Absolutely.'

"After the break, it was time for all participants to speak about themselves for about thirty to sixty seconds. These were not presentations, they were more like conversations the participants had with me, the trainer.

"When it was time for the Regional Sales Director to give his presentation, the meltdown began immediately. First, he became flushed in the face and turned beet red. Then he started sweating profusely, with sweat dripping from his face to the shoulders and lapels of his suit. While speaking, he stammered, and it became tough even to hear because he spoke so quietly. He soon started gasping for air, almost hyperventilating. The entire room was shocked at what we had witnessed. Right after his talk, we took a break, and I went over to speak to him. We walked outside the training room, and I asked him if he was ok. He said, 'I am one of those individuals who would prefer to die than to speak in front of the group. This challenge has haunted me my entire career, and it has stopped me from being promoted within my organization. I am being groomed to lead a new division, and if I cannot get over this phobia, I will not move forward, and my career is finished.'

"He then said, 'I am an extreme snow skier! I travel the world looking for the highest mountains and slopes to ski. I am not afraid of death. I am a thrill-seeker, and yet, this speaking in public is debilitating.' He pulled out his phone and showed a video of him careening straight down this tall mountain slope. His entire disposition of excitement related to this phobia transitioned to the excitement associated with exhilaration. Once I noticed that change in his temperament, I asked him if he would be willing to share his video with the rest of the class. So, we connected his phone to the projector and had him talk about the extreme skiing video from his chair. After playing the video, I asked him to come in front of the class without speaking and demonstrate how to ski coming down one of the steep mountain slopes. We then asked him to close his eyes and tell us the critical considerations a skier must take to conquer those steep mountain slopes. Finally, I asked him to remain demonstrating how to ski and to open his eyes and introduce himself. He completed his first presentation successfully. During the rest of the two days of this seminar, every time the Regional Sales Director presented his presentations, he showed us how to ski while delivering.

"The Sales Director demonstrated the three E's. Specifically, this Sales Director found his 'excited to share' by transitioning his passion for skiing and transferring that passion to another internal mountain many speakers need to overcome.

"We did speak later, and he told me that he still gets nervous presenting, but he has found a way to transition from a feeling of nervousness so that he could make it downhill when giving presentations."

Golf Partiers Talking To Engineers

Ken Beyersdorf, President of Dale Carnegie Arizona shares a story about an international sales meeting that had turned into a five-day-long golf party. Every year this company would bring in between 800–1,000 sales representatives with the intent that they would learn the latest technology. Twenty or so engineers would spend time preparing a presentation that no one wanted to be at. They just wanted to get through it so they could drink and play golf.

"We worked with the engineers to speak in layman's terms so that sales reps could understand the technology so they could sell it. We met with everyone individually and got a feel for where their performance gaps were. We developed competencies and taught them the format for presenting technical information. Then, the second phase was to take the format and create their presentation with their information. They practiced for two weeks, presented it, maximized the opportunity that they had pulled from the first lesson and made adjustments Perfect Practice makes Perfect. Otherwise Practice Makes Permanent.

"The engineers reported that it was the best interaction they ever had. After the presentation, the sales people were coming up asking questions. Sales people wanted to talk to engineers! They established credibility and opened up the relationship so that the sales people could come up afterward and ask questions. Through how they presented the information they changed the relationship and how the two groups could work together in order to be mutually successful."

I Earned The Right To Coach

Berit Friman, CEO of Dale Carnegie, Sweden shares how one of her clients earned the right to coach by starting her presentation with a powerful story.

"This was a technical retail company and we were coaching the senior management team for a presentation to gain investors. This presentation had to have lots of numbers and data and was at the risk of being dry and boring. But, investors are human, too! You want to help the investors get a feeling of your business.

"The CEO decided to share a story. 'It was a dark, raining, early Nordic morning. A terrible day for a store opening. "Who is going to come out in this weather?" I felt terrible because I know my staff worked very hard to get ready for this opening. So I got in my car and drove down there in the darkness and pouring rain. The closer I got to the store, the more my doubt increased. But when I got there, I was shocked. There was a huge line! People were standing in line in the rain and darkness and cold so that they could be part of the store opening. This story said something about the brand and customer desire to engage with it. It spoke to the investors powerfully because it came from a story into which they could insert themselves instead of a mere number on a slide.'"

Berit goes on to reveal, "The CEO dared to start his presentation with this story. I was worried that it was going to fail, but he showed courage to be personal and it made an impact. People are still talking about it."

Mark Fitzmaurice, Director and Master Trainer, Dale Carnegie UK says, "We have to be willing to take a risk in our presentations. You have to take a risk to be bold and engaging. Otherwise all the learning is for nothing. Learning is one part, but the time comes to execute what you've learned and that takes courage and boldness." If we always stay in our comfort zone, we never grow, and we stay stuck. Let's keep growing.

Evidence DEFEATS Doubt

Dale Carnegie created DEFEATS, an acronym that illustrates types of evidence to use in our talks to overcome doubt.

Demonstrations
Examples
Facts
Exhibits
Analogies
Testimonials
Statistics

Let's look a little more closely at each way to provide evidence.

Demonstrations: We can physically demonstrate a product, idea, or physical object's effectiveness or use. One example is Australian VP of Sales who rode up on stage on a Harley Davidson motorcycle to demonstrate how much he loved America.

Examples: When we give a concrete example of our ideas through real life stories, we bring the listener into the talk and give it life. "Here's an example of how this fire extinguisher saved the life of a family in the middle of the night . . ."

Facts: Facts are provable and repeatable. Very little can top facts as evidence. We use data to illustrate a point. When followed up with a story to illustrate the point, this can be very powerful.

Exhibits: Similar to the demonstration is an exhibit. When we hear the term "Exhibit A" we often think of an attorney in a courtroom holding up an object or a photograph that shows proof of something. When we use a physical object as an exhibit to make our point, it is a powerful anchor for memory.

Analogies: The comparison of the similarities between two dissimilar objects or ideas. For example, "just as a smooth takeoff and landing is critical to any successful airplane flight, a smooth opening and closing is critical to a successful presentation."

Testimonials: Testimonials are among the most powerful ways to defeat doubt and provide credibility. Humans are social creatures and when we hear or see someone else having a positive experience with something, we believe that we are more likely to have that positive experience as well. Whenever we purchase something or hire someone based on five star reviews, we acknowledge the power of testimonials in action. If we can't bring in people to speak live, then share a video. And if we can't do that, then use their words and names as part of our presentations.

Statistics: The selection of facts to strengthen a key point. For example, "four out of five dentists recommend sugar free gum." The facts by themselves are "four dentists recommend sugar free gum. One dentist doesn't." But that's not compelling. When combined as "four out of five," the recommendation is more powerful.

Statistics can be overused, so we need to use them with caution. If we simply cite a bunch of statistics, we risk losing the audience's attention. This is where knowing our audience makes a difference. If we are speaking to a group of engineers, scientists, accountants or other "left brain" people, we can use more numbers and statistics. If we are speaking to a more intuitive audience, then statistics should be used sparingly. Remember that merely showing a bunch of data isn't enough. We need to help people interpret the data and "connect the dots" to the message. Rather than hoping people will figure out what the statistics mean, help them follow the trail to the answer so that they don't reach the "wrong" conclusion.

A blog post from Dale Carnegie of Long Beach and Southern Los Angeles explains it this way.*

A central framework for making your case in any context is your ability to use evidence. Here are the seven principles we teach that will help you use evidence to DEFEAT doubt.

1. D = Demonstrations
If you've ever been captivated by a late night infomercial or found yourself purchasing something you just saw demon-

---

* https://www.dalecarnegielosangeles.com/single-post/2015/01/12/how-to-use-evidence
-to-defeat-doubt

strated at a store or conference, you already know the power of using demonstrations.

You can speak all day long about how great your idea, software, or service is, but it pales in comparison to showing people exactly how something works. When you do, they can picture how they could use it, fund it, or market it to their customers. If practical, involve your audience in the demonstration too.

2. E = Examples

Telling stories about who has benefitting from your idea, product, or service is one of the best ways to use examples, another form of evidence.

The key with storytelling is to keep the example focused on a single incident, followed by a clear action and benefit. We teach a process called the Magic Formula (funny name, but powerful concept) to do this effectively. (We'll cover the Magic Formula later in this book.)

3. F = Facts

In order for something to be a useful fact, it should be both verifiable and indisputable. Making a claim that your team or company is "the best in the industry" is rarely verifiable and always disputed by the competition.

Instead, highlight facts that are easy to verify and can't be argued. When speaking about our own organization, we often highlight that Dale Carnegie has been in business since 1912. Without saying a word about credibility and sustainability, that fact communicates all of that, while being easy for others to verify.

4. E = Exhibits

The United Nations in engaged with a project called the GIFT (Global Initiative to Fight Human Trafficking) box in order to teach people about this issue. These physical boxes travel all over the world and serve as walk-in exhibits, personalized for each community. The connections that come from attendees at these events often build partnerships that raise awareness throughout the local area.

It's a fantastic example of using an exhibit to get an important message across. An exhibit is a static display that helps you make your case to the world.

5. A = Analogies

If you're about to make the case for something that's hard to understand, employ an analogy. It connects what you are trying to explain with something the audience already knows, without you having to point out that they know less about something than you do (rarely a good idea).

Start with something that most everyone understands and use it to explain the complex part. Years ago, one of our clients at Exxon Mobil did this beautifully. We had asked how different grades of gasoline were made and he compared it to eating chips and salsa at a Mexican restaurant.

"If you have hot sauce and mild sauce on the table, how do you make medium?" he asked. Mixing them together was the obvious answer. "That's how we make the mid grade gasoline," he replied. "We make only a high and low grade at the refinery, and mix them together to get the mid grade."

6. T = Testimonials

When you are making a case for something, one of the questions always lurking in the back of the mind of the other party (whether they verbalize it or not) is this one:

Who says so other than just you?

Of course you're going to speak well about the case you are making, since you're the one making it. You add credibility to your argument when you bring in a testimonial from another party. Who's the person to mention?

Here are the two rules for who to get a testimonial from:

1. Someone who has experience with your product or service.
2. Someone who is seen by your audience as credible.

The second rule is often missed. Just because someone said something nice about your idea, service, or organization doesn't mean your audience will be impressed. Highlighting testimonials that the audience sees as credible is key.

7. S = Statistics

Statistics follow the same rules as facts, but normally include numbers and trends. There's an old adage about statistics you should know about too:

There are three kinds of lies: lies, damn lies, and statistics.

So many people and organizations skew numbers to help support their case, that you must be ever vigilant if you plan to use statistics successfully. Here are three guidelines:

1. Ensure they are easily understood
2. Reference a credible source (in the audience's eyes) where the numbers come from
3. Provide an easy way for the audience to verify the source

Dos and Don'ts of Demonstrating Credibility

DO know your material so well that you own it.

DO know more about your subject than you'll need for your talk

DO use visuals as aids.

DO be yourself

DO use evidence to defeat doubt

DO use full names and titles

DON'T use jargon and acronyms

DON'T write out your whole presentation. If you do write out some notes, only use them as reference

DON'T open with a joke

DON'T use visuals AS your presentation

DON'T be something or someone you're not

The single best thing we can do for improving our presentation skill is to practice. Practice out loud. Practice with a live audience. And practice until we have done it properly. Why do so many people think speaking is different from any other art form? No one would try to play the violin in public without years of training. No one would play in public until they had mastered the piece of music. Speaking is no different, so taking the time to rehearse is an essential step.

In this chapter, we covered the Three Es of establishing credibility and the DEFEATS acronym for dispelling doubt. In the next chapter, we'll cover the final topic in the trust formula—Empathy.

Thoughts from a Master: Brenda Wells, Dale Carnegie of Orange County, California

"If you had one piece of advice to share with someone who wants to be a better public speaker, what would it be?"

Embrace the nerves. Along the way people think that if they are not nervous that means that they are a good public speaker. Those are the worst public speakers! They don't prepare, lean into their own confidence, or think about how they feel versus the audience. They take the process for granted. Not being nervous does not mean you're a good speaker. Being nervous drives preparation.

From Dale Carnegie Himself

Once a group of our instructors were asked to write on a slip of paper what they considered was the biggest problem they had with beginning speakers. When the slips were tallied, it was found that "getting beginners to talk on the right topic" was the problem most frequently encountered in early sessions of my course. What is the right topic? You can be sure you have the right topic for you if you have lived with it, made it your own through experience and reflection. How do you find topics? By dipping into your memory and searching your background for those significant aspects of your life that made a vivid impression on you.

Several years ago, we made a survey of topics that held the attention of listeners in our classes. We found that the topics most approved by the audience were concerned with certain fairly defined areas of one's background: Early Years and Upbringing. Topics that deal with the family, childhood memories, schooldays, invariably get attention, because most of us are interested in the way other people met and overcame obstacles in the environment in which they were reared. Whenever possible, work into your talks, illustrations and examples from your early years. The popularity of plays, movies, and stories that deal with the subject of meeting the challenges of the world in one's early years attests to the value of this area for subject matter of talks.

But how can you be sure anyone will be interested in what happened to you when you were young? There's one test. If something stands out vividly in your memory after many years have gone by, that almost guarantees that it will be of interest to an audience.

Early Struggles to Get Ahead.

This is an area rich in human interest. Here again the attention of a group can be held by recounting your first attempts to make your mark on the world. How did you get into a particular job or profession? What twist of circumstances accounted for your career? Tell us about your setbacks, your hopes, your triumphs when you were establishing yourself in the competitive world. A real-life picture of almost anyone's life—if told modestly—is almost surefire material.

Hobbies and Recreation.

Topics in this area are based on personal choice and, as such, are subjects that command attention. You can't go wrong talking about something you do out of sheer enjoyment. Your natural enthusiasm for your particular hobby will help get this topic across to any audience.

Special Areas of Knowledge.

Many years of working in the same field have made you an expert in your line of endeavor. You can be certain of respectful attention if you discuss aspects of your job or profession based on years of experience or study.

Unusual Experiences.

Have you ever met a great man? Were you under fire during the war? Have you gone through a spiritual crisis in your life? These are experiences that make the best kind of speech material.

Beliefs and Convictions.

Perhaps you have given a great deal of time and effort to thinking about your position on vital subjects confronting the world today. If you have devoted many hours to the study of issues of importance, you have earned the right to talk about them. But when you do, be certain that you give specific instances for your convictions. Audiences do not relish a talk filled with generalizations. Please don't consider the casual reading of a few newspaper articles sufficient preparation to talk on these topics. If you know little more about a subject than the people in your audience, it is best to avoid it. On the other hand, if you have devoted years of study to some subject, it is undoubtedly a topic that is made to order for you. By all means, use it.

6: EMPATHY

Mark Cahill was practicing his talk on his wife. After going through his opening and sharing the facts and evidence that demonstrated credibility, he was just about to go into his closing when his wife stopped him. "Mark, I get everything you're saying and agree that the facts make a lot of sense. However, you're missing one thing. Why should they CARE? What's missing is a sense of. . . . empathy, or even rapport. What you're presenting appeals to the left side/logic side of the brain. What about the human side?"

Recall that The Trust Formula is:

Trust = Credibility + Empathy

The second component, Empathy, is about connecting with our audience. It's about tuning in to what they need to hear in the moment and then connecting to that.

Dave Wright, CEO of Dale Carnegie Training Houston, Austin, San Antonio, shares a very personal story. "We had a very dear team member who'd been on board with us since 2008. She was literally the backbone of our sales team. In 2018, she had a series of strokes and couldn't work. It was devastating to all of us. In January of 2019, I was trying to have my first team meeting after this happened. I spent at least a day thinking about the first hour. In thinking about the presentation to my team, I asked myself, 'Where is my team right now (emotionally wrecked) and where do I want them to end up (feeling okay that we can make it work).'

"I had to meet them where they were, and then planned a presentation to move from wanting to hold hands and cry to being able to move to 'okay we are going to go make it work.' Our team had to step up. I started with a video that met them where they were, emotionally, and then talked about my feelings and that they were okay. I asked them, 'Is our vision still our vision? Does it still inspire us? What would she want us to do? How do we fill it? I then finished with action items.'"

How did Dave manage to get his team through such an emotional crisis? By focusing on THEM and what THEY needed. Another manager might have just powered through to the business with a perfunctory acknowledgment of the missing team member. And it would have likely blown up, either during or after the meeting. When we don't address what is on people's minds, they can't focus on anything else. And we miss our opportunity for them to hear our message.

Key social skills

Key social skills are among the most important abilities a person can have.

When giving presentations, why is it that some people make such a positive impression? What behaviors actually imprint a person on our memory to the point where that person is unforgettable—while there are other people whom we can't forget soon enough? What are the actual behaviors that define someone as a confident class act? The answers are found in five key social skills.

These are among the most important abilities a person can have. And while these abilities are inborn in a certain percentage of people, they can also be learned.

Relax

The first of the social skills is not really anything we do, but how we feel. It's the capacity to *relax* in a social or business setting. Stress and anxiety are contagious. When we seem ill at ease, that feeling is transmitted to others around us in what scientists call "emotional contagion." Yes! Emotions are contagious. If we seem confident and composed, there's a good chance we'll encounter that same state of mind in everyone else. In developing the ability to relax, the first step is to remember that it's not about the speaker! As we've said before in this book, when we shift the focus from "What will they think of me?" to "How can I connect with them?" We tend to relax because we're not focused on our nervousness, we're focused on serving them.

Without overly dramatizing our feelings, we can just mention that we're sometimes a bit uneasy meeting new people or speaking in public. This can create a sense of empathy in the audience, as almost all of us can relate to being nervous in front of a group. The main point is to be upfront about the issue (without apologizing!) and thereby defuse it. Rest assured that nobody is going to hold this against us. In fact, admitting these very human feelings is a great way to get people on our side.

Keep in mind also that certain actions act as triggers for anxiety, even though we may think they're calming us down. We should try not to do anything too quickly, whether it's walking, talking, eating, or even sitting down in a chair. Rapid, jerky motions awaken a primitive fight-or-flight syndrome that's the last thing we want. We should take our time. Subvocally, we can tell ourselves to relax. We may be surprised at the heightened level of confidence we'll feel, and the positive effect it will have on others around us.

Listen

So the ability to relax is the first social skill of a confident person—and the second of the key social skills is closely related to it. It's the *ability to listen*. People who are ill at ease often have a habit of talking too much, too fast, or too loud. It's a misdirected attempt to take control of the situation—because they're afraid of what might happen if they don't. The sad part is, it's extremely annoying to be around a person when we can't get a word in edgewise.

Listen carefully. Sometimes opportunity knocks quietly. Even when we are speaking in front of a group, we can listen. Listen to the energy in the room. Listen to see if the audience is paying attention or if they are bored. Ask questions and listen to the answers.

Aubrey Percy was invited to speak at a conference of food manufacturing plant managers about innovation on the first day of their three day conference. Although she had presented the topic successfully many times before, the audience was not responsive. They were a "cold audience!" She could almost hear the crickets chirping when she asked the audience for an answer to a question. Since she was listening to the energy from the group, she pivoted and cut out the participative parts of the presentation since they were not going over well. She managed to get through the rest of her presentation successfully. When she asked a meeting organizer about it after her presentation, she found out that the next speaker was going to talk about the reorganization of their manufacturing division. Of course the audience wasn't paying attention, they were worried for their jobs! No one thought to mention this to Aubrey, nor did she think to ask.

Empathy

As we're listening to the audience, we can tap into the third skill of confident interaction. This is *empathy and genuine interest* in the experiences of our group. Training ourselves to really feel what someone is trying to communicate is probably the quickest way to make ourselves truly unforgettable—maybe just because it's so rare.

Here's a simple rule that can help us develop empathy very quickly. It involves recognizing a certain very common interpersonal behavior and making a conscious decision to eliminate it. I'm referring to the game of "Topper." You may never have heard of this contest, but there's an excellent chance that you've played it anyway. And if you haven't, there's an even better chance that it's been played on you.

Very simply, here's how Topper works. Someone tells a story—it's usually something that happened to the speaker. When they're done, we tell a story about ourself that tops the first one as a way of "one-upping" them. It's so simple and natural to do. Maybe that's why it fills up so many conversations, the consequence is that it kills empathy with the speaker. Perhaps that's also why so few people have any sense of a real empathic connection.

Topper is such a seductive game that we can actually see people struggling to hold back until they can start talking about themselves. Do we think these people are really listening? Do we think they're building a connection? Nope. When we are interacting with individuals in our audience, resist the urge to "top" what they are saying and turn the focus back to us.

Rapport

Empathy is a feeling. *Rapport,* our fourth of the key social skills, is the outward expression of that feeling. When we feel empathy, we act so as to build rapport. Rapport is a state of understanding or connection that happens in a social interaction. It basically says "I am like you; we understand each other." Rapport occurs on an unconscious level, and when it happens, the language, speech patterns, body movement and posture, and other aspects of communication can synchronize down to incredibly fine levels.

Jonathan Vehar, former Vice President of Product for Dale Carnegie recalls a presentation with MBA students where he was having the audience clasp their hands in a specific way to make a point about habits. In the middle of this activity, one of the participants fell out of her chair and had a grand mal seizure. It was clear that those around her didn't know what to do. Jonathan recalled his first aid training, and directed one student to call 911 to get emergency responders to the room and followed proper protocol while clearing the room. After the paramedics responded and treated the woman, Jonathan had one of the paramedics do an impromptu training session about how to treat someone having a seizure, and then gave the students an opportunity to ask questions—Yes, she'll be okay. People who have seizures recover and typically feel exhausted and irritable. Yes, she'll probably return to the program tomorrow. No, the hand-clasping activity does not cause seizures—After that, the group returned to the content at hand and proceeded without incident. In this situation, Jonathan picked up on the feelings of helplessness, concern, and fear from the group that arose from helplessly standing by while one of their own had a seizure, and took the time to help the group process those feelings as well as he could—enlisting the support of the paramedics to educate before helping to process the emotions.

Rapport is an unconscious process, and it can be encouraged by conscious efforts. One way is by mirroring or matching the verbal behavior of the other person. It's nothing complicated—just reflecting back language and speech mannerisms, including rate, volume, tone, and choice of words. Sometimes, when two people feel good about each other, this happens all by itself. Rapport has taken place spontaneously. Other times the mirroring technique is a good way to create rapport where it would otherwise be absent.

An important sub-category of building rapport is appropriate eye contact. This doesn't mean we have to stare at people—in fact, staring at someone can communicate anger—maintaining eye contact while talking or listening is a matter of basic civility. It simply shows them that they have our undivided attention. We're focused on them and what they have to say.

If we don't maintain eye contact, several ideas can pass through people's minds—and none of them are positive. They may think we're ignoring them or that we're trying to get away from them. If they have any worries about their own confidence, this is sure to bring them on in a painful way. People like this will blame themselves for the lack of rapport. If we've failed to even look them in the eye, it's really us who should be taking responsibility.

People need to receive attention—and they need to give it also. Listen empathically to what others say, and then share similar ideas and concerns of our own. We need to not overwhelm someone with our own drama—don't play Topper—but by the same token, we should not be so reserved that we seem aloof.

People need a sense of meaning, purpose, and goals. If we're a manager in a corporate setting or a business owner, satisfying this need is a basic element of confident leadership. Whatever they may tell us or whatever they may think, no one works just for money—at least not for very long. When we help fulfill others' purpose and goals, we'll reach ours.

Status

Finally, people need a sense of status. As a confident person and as a class act, we are in a unique position to confer feelings of recognition and importance. This can take many forms. Sometimes it means singling someone out for praise in front of a group. Other times it's taking someone aside to offer thanks for a job well done. When we apply these five key social skills in our personal and professional life, we'll radiate power, and in its reflection we'll shine brightly.

The bottom line is, once again, Dale Carnegie's Principle #17: "Try honestly to see things from the other person's point of view." To do that we need to be aware of others and focus on them. Not on ourselves. Jonathan Vehar was delivering a presentation to 250 deans of university business schools from around the country on February 1, 2003. During the break, people started to hear news reports that the Space Shuttle Columbia had exploded upon re-entry to the earth's atmosphere. The conference organizers discussed what to do, with options ranging from canceling the rest of the meeting to encouraging Jonathan not to mention it and to keep going with the presentation. The team decided to continue the meeting. When the meeting resumed after the break, Jonathan shared with the audience what had happened and what was known about the situation. And then he called a moment of silence, a feeling he says he'll "never forget." The audience was then encouraged to take care of what they needed to do for their own well-being, and if necessary they were told they could leave the presentation. No one left, everyone took a deep breath, and the presentation continued. Jonathan put himself in the place of the audience members, and remembered how devastated he felt when the space shuttle Challenger blew up 17 years earlier. He opted to give people the information they needed and the power to make the decision to stay or go based on their needs. Members of the audience appreciated this approach which put the information and decision in their hands, demonstrating both empathy and trust in their ability to do what they needed to do for themselves.

In this chapter, we talked about how to create empathy with and from your audience. This, combined with credibility are the formula for building trust as a speaker.

In Part Three of the book, we'll delve into the actual delivery of the presentation.

Thoughts from a Master: Rebecca Collier, Global Master Trainer

If you had one piece of advice to share with someone who wants to be a better public speaker, what would it be?

I would tell you to check your ego and focus on who your listeners are. So much of the work I do is based on getting people over the fear and horror of public speaking but it's also about getting over the need to perform and create a persona. It's not about you but who you are communicating with. Too often we are focused on ourselves. "How do I look?" "How do I sound?" Instead, work on knowing your audience, your subject. What are the skepticisms and resistances? What's the takeaway? Focus the presentation and delivery from their perspective.

From Dale Carnegie Himself

There are three factors in every speaking situation: the speaker, the speech or the message, and the audience. The first two parts of this book dealt with the interrelationships of the speaker to a speech. Up to this point there is no speaking situation. Only when the speaker relates his talk to a living audience will the speaking situation come to life. The talk may be well prepared; it may concern a topic which the speaker is excited about; but for complete success, another factor must enter into his delivery of the talk. He must make his listeners feel that what he has to say is important to them. He must not only be excited about his topic, but he must be eager to transfer this excitement to his listeners. In every public speaker of note in the history of eloquence, there has been this unmistakable quality of salesmanship, evangelism, call it what you will. The effective speaker earnestly desires his listeners to feel what he feels, to agree with his point of view, to do what he thinks is right for them to do, and to enjoy and relive his experience with him. He is audience-centered and not self-centered. He knows that the success or failure of his talk is not for him to decide—it will be decided in the minds and hearts of his hearers.

Part Three

Delivery

For years, there was a certain amount of resistance on the part of some people who didn't want to read *How to Win Friends and Influence People*. Before actually reading the book, those people felt that the topic was manipulative and more akin to "How to Get People To Do What You Want Them To Do."

Once those people actually read the book, though, they discovered the truth. The book isn't about how to get other people to do your bidding. It's about how we can become the kind of person that people like and want to help. How? By being interested in other people and paying attention to their needs.

It's the same thing in public speaking. The goal of this book isn't to give you the tools and tricks to get an audience to do what you want them to do. It's about becoming the kind of speaker who focuses on the listener and gives them a message they need to hear in a way that resonates with them.

As the speaker, you are the message, and it's not about you. It's about the listener.

Thus far in *SPEAK! How to Get Over the Fear and Horror of Public Speaking*, we've talked about the things to do before we ever set foot on stage. The rest of the book will be dedicated to the actual delivery of our messages. This includes crafting a positive first impression, specific presentation competencies, telling effective stories, and how to overcome things like stage fright.

7: CREATING A POSITIVE FIRST IMPRESSION

"They're ready for you, Mr. Cahill," the receptionist said as she opened the double glass doors.

As he stood up to follow her in, Mark thought he might throw up. His head got light and all he could hear were the voices of doubt in his head. "What makes you think you'll have anything interesting to say? Don't you remember that speech class you took in high school? They literally laughed at you."

"Mr. Cahill?" The woman stood at the door, looking at him expectantly.

"Well, I can't get out of it now," Mark thought as he swallowed his nerves and headed into the conference room where the executive team sat waiting for him. "Let's get this over with."

Mark walked through the glass doors and entered a conference room with a long table filled with the C-Suite exec-

utives whose names he'd only seen on company documents, along with all of their key lieutenants. Although his heart was pounding and he felt nervous, he also knew that he was ready for this presentation. He'd spent weeks planning every aspect of this talk. All he could do was try his best, and focus on the audience.

He took a deep breath, stood tall, looked around the room and made eye contact with each person in the room before speaking.

"When I was a little boy, my grandfather used to take me fishing every Sunday. As we sat there, silently, watching the sun rise over the glassy lake, my grandfather would tell me, 'Mark . . . catching fish is a lot like . . .'"

There's an old saying, "You never get a second chance to make a first impression." All too often, we think that our first impression is the first thing we say to an audience. In reality, they start to make their minds up about us when they first enter the room. It starts with the room setup. Does it look professional, or did people just move some chairs out of the way for us to talk? Then, the next thing people notice is our introduction. Are we being introduced by someone else? If so, what are they saying? Finally, they are looking at our appearance. Not our level of attractiveness, our hair or outfit or the things we are worried they are noticing. They're looking at our posture, our confident expression, our body language, and the "vibe" we're giving off.

The Introduction

In many cases, although not every one, the audience is "introduced" to the speaker—either by him or herself or by another person. Whenever given the chance, we should craft our own introduction—especially if it's being spoken by another person. Why? Because then we can be sure to include things that are relevant to the audience. Remember that everything that is said about us becomes part of the audience's expectation of how the presentation is going to go.

Here are some things to consider when creating your introduction.

1. Why you? What makes you an expert in the subject?
2. Why this subject? Why should the audience care about the topic?
3. Why this audience? How is the topic relevant to this specific audience at this specific time?

We shouldn't waste words on things that aren't relevant to the subject of our talk. We may be a world class pastry chef with many pastry awards to our credit. But if we're giving a talk to a group of veterinarians on the use of grain in dog foods, our expertise as a pastry chef isn't relevant. Be concise!

When we are giving our own introduction, resist the temptation to use that as our opening. The most boring opening line is "Hello, my name is . . ." We must avoid that at all costs! As we discovered earlier in the book, having a powerful opening can immediately draw the reader into our talk. Starting out with our name and bio is a sure-fire way to lose that momentum early on. Instead, we should start with our planned opening and then back up into our introduction.

"You might be wondering how I know this . . ."

Another aspect of the first impression is our body language. It's a subconscious message that the audience picks up on that tells them how we feel about being there. Blair Miller, a speaker and trainer, talks about his "Starting Stance," head up, shoulders back, straight posture and beginning with a warm, loud, clear voice. Even if we're not trained to have military-straight posture always, this initial impression is what sticks

The Dashboard Hula Dancer

Brenda Wells of Dale Carnegie Orange County shares a story about how body language can add to or detract from our credibility—before we even say a word! "There was a young woman in our course, standing in front of the room. You could tell she was nervous by the way she was standing. Her legs were practically melded together! From her ankles to her knees, they were one. She ended up being off balance, giving her a kind of 'dashboard hula dancer' sway. Before she spoke, I walked up to her and gave her a gentle push on one shoulder. She stumbled over to the side! I then told her to try widening her stance eight inches. She did it and I pushed again. She didn't move.

"Now, this may seem like a small detail, however, it was a powerful visual metaphor. She was conveying that she was so much stronger in her position, not a pushover.

Home base is where you are standing your ground. *I am standing my ground*. Literal and symbolic. Stable in presenting. It takes a little while for the feeling to catch up and it definitely affects your credibility with the audience."

Be Congruent With Your Message

Rebecca Collier, Global Master Trainer shares a powerful example of how we need to be congruent with our message to our audience. "One of the most memorable people I ever worked with in training, Ray, came to us through vocational rehabilitation and had lost an arm. He was working on regaining his self confidence. During one presentation he was giving, we could sense his discomfort and he was not making eye contact. He kept rubbing where his arm had been.

"We had a conversation that was focused on this. 'What's going on in your mind?' I asked.

"'I just feel like I'm not all here,' he answered, looking at his feet. My heart swelled in empathy for him. 'You are so here in this space,' I reassured him. 'We just need you to connect with us. If you trust me, talk to only me . . .'

"One technique we use in training is to close the space between the trainer and the presenter. He started talking only to and stopped rubbing his shoulder. His voice got stronger and his stance got secure. I moved back out of the way so that he was then talking to the group. Sometimes, when we get on our feet to talk, we feel there's something missing and we don't have something valuable to say. Each of us can compensate for that perceived missing piece if we take a risk. Ray's smile was triumphant, reassuring, relieved, and his talk became a moment for him where he proved something to himself."

Eye Contact Is Crucial

Effective speakers know how to use visual stimuli to enhance what they have to say. So let's not just reach our listeners through their ears. Eye contact is also a hugely important way of connecting. When we speak, it's really our eyes that involve our listeners in our presentation. And on the other side of the coin, there's no surer way to break the bond between us and the audience than by failing to look at our listeners. Remember: our listeners have their eyes on us. More specifically, they have their eyes on our eyes. So we should take advantage of that fact to connect with them.

What To Wear

Every detail of what we wear should be the result of a conscious decision on our part—because at the end of our speech, there may be some people who don't know what we said, but virtually all of them will know what kind of shoes we were wearing or whether our tie was crooked. So we need to make sure that every item of our clothing is clean and well-tailored. Don't wear jewelry that might glitter or jingle when you move or gesture. And most importantly, we should try to dress in a way that matches the style and level of our listeners' attire. As with eye contact, it's amazing how often this basic tactical principle is ignored—so as we're preparing our speech, we should spend a moment or two in front of a full-length mirror in the outfit we intend to wear. It's a chance to be proud of how great we look. And it might also be a chance to save ourselves some embarrassment. After giving a presentation in Brazil to a group of managers, Cam Robertson was speaking to a participant who had approached him. During the conversion, that participant said, "I saw your highly polished shoes and knew you were the real deal." Cam can also tell you about the time he began a presentation with his fly open because he was running late. Details matter.

The Way You Move

The way we move in front of the audience—or whether we move at all should be a matter of conscious choice, and it should start at the moment after we're introduced. We should walk briskly, purposefully, confidently, and calmly to our speaking position. We should have a real smile on our face, or at least a pleasant expression. Even if we're terrified of what we're about to do, we must try to breathe and relax. Initially, we don't yet look at the audience. We should look instead at the person who has just introduced us and greet that person with a handshake and a word of thanks. Then we pause, arrange our notes if we have any, and finally turn our gaze toward our listeners.

Think of the initial position behind the lectern as our home base. Now identify two other positions as alternative bases. As our talk progresses, we're going to be moving among those three locations, and only those three locations. Further, our movements should be dictated by the content of our material, not just by our desire to take a stroll. Just as when we consult our notes, moving from one point to another can give our listeners a chance to absorb what we've just said—or it can provide an infusion of energy for a point we're about to make.

Three Tips for Making a Great First Impression

1. Let's not just aim to make our speech interesting—let's make it the most interesting speech our audience has ever heard. It's not that difficult. All we have to do is talk about the subject that our audience finds more fascinating than any other. (Hint: It's themselves.)
2. We should express genuine, sincere appreciation for the opportunity to address our listeners
3. Immediately break down the distinction between ourselves and the audience. As soon as possible, perhaps even with the first words out of our mouths, we should indicate some direct relationship with the group we're addressing.

My Wife Wanted To Know What Happened To Me

Tina Graziotto, Vice President of Program Management and Instruction at Dale Carnegie Training of Western and Central Pennsylvania shares a story of how seeing ourselves as others see us can change everything. "He was a Vice President of a global steel manufacturing company (operations) with more than a thousand employees. He was a typical middle-aged guy—a very imposing figure, and when he came to the program he was very intimidating. After the first day, my coaching was to have fun, lighten up, don't take it so seriously. 'Have fun and smile,' I said.

"He came back the second day. 'My wife wanted to know what happened to me. She could tell there was something different and that you were coaching me to smile more. She told me, I have been telling you for thirty years to smile more.' The whole point was that he finally realized how his audience previously saw him—that he was completely unapproachable. For him, this was about so much more than giving a presentation. This had to do with his leadership. He had been coming off as unapproachable and intimidating. Changing his facial expressions changed that."

Thoughts from a Master: Nancy Covert, President of Dale Carnegie Training of Birmingham and Huntsville, Alabama

If you had one piece of advice to share with someone who wants to be a better public speaker, what would it be?

One of the biggest things we do when we teach High Impact Presentations every week is teach people you have to have the right attitude and mindset. You can't go into it thinking, "I hate public speaking. I am going to look like an idiot."

Say positive things out loud to get a positive mindset. When people stop thinking about themselves the message can come through.

My dear colleague Pam Wilkes came up with a great visual illustration of this concept. It's a rope tied in a knot to help you remember, "It's knot about you."

From Dale Carnegie Himself

NEVER MEMORIZE A TALK WORD FOR WORD. By "perfect preparation" do I mean that you should memorize your talk? To this question I give back a thunderous NO. In their attempts to protect their egos from the dangers of drawing a mental blank before an audience, many speakers fall headlong into the trap of memorization. Once a victim of this type of mental dope addiction, the speaker is hopelessly bound to a time-consuming method of preparation that destroys effectiveness on the platform.

If we memorize our talk word for word, we will probably forget it when we face our listeners. Even if we do not forget our memorized talk, we will probably deliver it, in a mechanical way. Why? Because it will not come from our hearts, but from our memories. When talking with people privately, we always think of something we want to say, and then we go ahead and say it without thinking of words. We have been doing that all our lives. Why attempt to change it now?

I have heard countless scores of men and women try to deliver memorized talks, but I don't remember even one speaker who wouldn't have been more alive, more effective, more human, if he had tossed his memorized talk into the waste baskets. If he had done that, he might have forgotten some of his points. He might have rambled. But at least he would have been human.

8: PRESENTATION COMPETENCIES

Mark Cahill felt like his opening had gone well. He had the attention of everyone in the room and they all chuckled at the right place in his story with his grandfather. He'd come prepared with a Powerpoint presentation and was about to hit the start button. He'd practiced this presentation so many times at home, but this was for real. "Don't read from the slides," he told himself silently. "You know this stuff. Just be conversational." "How many of you have ever seen the piece of technology that we're talking about today? Raise your hands if you've ever seen one of . . . these."

When we think of "tips" on public speaking, the ideas contained in this chapter are generally the first things that come to mind. Things like oral communication skills, body language, and how to effectively use visual aids are the kinds of content included in every book and course on public speaking.

As we've discovered, however, our view is quite a bit deeper. We've been advocating that it's important to be authentic in our communication. The tips and strategies we'll discover here are not intended to make us into some grand orator. Instead, they'll help us be more effective at communicating our messages. Again, it's not about YOU and how well you speak. It's about the listener and how easy it will be for them to receive your ideas. It's what makes the difference between being a credible speaker and one who is not.

Verbal Competencies

Verbal competency relates to how well we use our voice and words to communicate ideas. Often, we aren't aware of how we come off to others when we are speaking. Things like volume, our accents, where we place emphasis on certain words can affect the meaning and interpretation of our presentation.

Voice Modulation
Practice saying the following sentences aloud, stressing the bold and italicized words. Note the different meanings conveyed.
1. You can *never* put too many cherries in a Coke.
2. You can never put *too many* cherries in a Coke
3. You can never put too many *cherries* in a Coke.
4. You can never put too many cherries *in a Coke.*

The first sentence implies that it's bad or dangerous to put too many cherries in a coke. The second sentence implies that no matter how many cherries are in a Coke, it is not too many. The third sentence implies that of all the things you can put in a Coke, cherries are delicious (but don't add Brussels sprouts). The last one implies that you wouldn't want to put a lot of cherries in another beverage, such as root beer.

Pitch

Varying the pitch in our voice can convey meaning as well. For example, say the following sentence using a high pitched voice (as we would talk to a baby, or a pet), your normal pitch, and a low pitch.

"Come here."

When said in a high pitched voice, "Come here" sounds like a request. When said in a lower pitched voice, it sounds like a command or even a threat.

Volume

How loud we speak can be an unconscious pattern or it can be used with intent to create mood and dramatic tension. Speaking loudly or softly can be a great way to bring the audience's attention back if they've started to wander. The variation in volume brings the listener's attention back to us, occasionally, when we want to emphasize a point, we can speak more quietly which makes people work to listen. That's a way to regain their attention. But only occasionally.

Let's Get Loud

Andreas Iffland, Carnegie Master in Germany, shares an anecdote about this. "A senior manager of a global company was at one of our training sessions. The CEO was in the room, and the manager was feeling nervous. He was a technical engineer—very data driven, and when he was presenting in front of the group he tended to speak very softly. I coached him on talking louder. After some time, he replied very loudly, 'SHOULD I SHOUT AT YOU?' I answered, loudly, 'YES!' While he didn't shout during the presentation, he was not the same soft-spoken engineer, and he conveyed confidence. In the end, he got a standing ovation. It went great." If we don't push ourselves out of our comfort zone when practicing, then we'll shrink back to their comfort zone during the presentation. And that's not where we're most effective when we're speaking.

Speed

So many effects can be achieved by varying the speed of our words. As an example, say "thirty million dollars" very fast, as if that were a trivial sum of money.

Then say, "Thirrrrttttyyyy millllionnnn dollllarrrsss," extending every syllable to the maximum. Now it really seems like a lot of money. By increasing the time you took to say it, it's almost as if you've increased the amount itself. Yet the actual words you've spoken are just the same.

It Was Like A Different Language

Tina Graziotto, Vice President of Program Management and Instruction at Dale Carnegie Training of Western and Central Pennsylvania shares a story that illustrates how effective it can be to change the speed with which we are speaking.

"I worked with an IT project manager for a regional insurance company who was originally from India and English was his second language. He tended to speak quickly and through clenched teeth making him hard for people from the US to understand. During the course of our program I helped him learn to open his mouth more widely, round out words and let the words come out. When he did this, his credibility changed. Before he came to the program, people weren't always sure what he was saying, which led to lack of credibility. The transformation was dramatic. It was like he was speaking a different language. His credibility increased significantly!"

Shifting Out Of Performance Mode

In another example, Rebecca Collier, Global Master Trainer talks about the danger of being in "performance mode."

"A young woman, Katie, had a lot of theater background, and during our training, when she was in front of the room, she was 'always on.' But it was artificial. You could sense she put out a lot of information, but we didn't have authentic engagement. It was about performing. I challenged her to trust that it would be okay for her to let us get to know her real authentic self. She was not excited about that idea, but I challenged her to see what would happen if she shifted gears. 'Katie let us see you.' Pause. Reset. Her body language relaxed into the spot she was holding in front of the group. Suddenly, she became relatable, transparent, honest, and vulnerable. She discovered that it was okay to be vulnerable when giving a talk. This was more than twenty years ago and we are still in touch. She internalized this message and it changed how she interacts with others.

"So often, we have these great insights and authentic observations, but when we stand up we can lose them. We put on a different persona when we are speaking. Don't do that. It masks insecurities."

Nonverbal

One of the best examples of how nonverbal communication can get the audience involved comes from Southwest Airlines. Robert Korp, Director of Training Quality EMEA for Dale Carnegie recalls a viral video from a few years ago. "You remember the video that a passenger took on a Southwest Airlines flight where the flight attendant made the safety briefing funny and engaging? This person was asked by the CEO of Southwest to come and give the financial report to the shareholders! Talk about bringing passion and love to something otherwise boring. It was 'stomp, clap, stomp, clap . . .' Everyone was uplifted and felt inspired."

Don't just think about our words conveying our authentic selves, we should also use our nonverbals to demonstrate our passion, our enthusiasm, or the action that occurred in the story. If we're talking about how we crossed the room in the restaurant to say, "hello," to someone, then walk across the space and hold out our hand as if to shake hands with the person. If we're talking about a large machine, indicate its size with our hands.

Stance and Deliver

Brenda Wells from Dale Carnegie of Orange County shares a story of how stance can affect the audience's perception of us. "In another class, we had a retired marine and he had a wide stance. You can imagine him standing up there with his hands behind back. It was the classic Restrained Warrior pose. His feet were too wide and he thought he was giving the impression, 'I'm strong and in charge.' He was smiling, but the body language was conveying, 'Don't get too close. It's not safe.' That wasn't the image he wanted to project at all!

"So, we shifted his stance to have his weight bearing on one leg and one hand in his pocket. This one minor change made him instantly more relatable and approachable."

Smile And The World Smiles With You

Andreas Iffland, Carnegie Master in Germany shares a powerful story about how a smile can change everything. "A Managing Director of a company in Switzerland was presenting and I saw the video from the other room. 'This guy needs to smile more,' I thought. I went into the other room and pushed him to smile. 'I'm smiling already,' he said. I said, 'No you're not.' He thought he was smiling but he wasn't. 'What could be some reasons you're not smiling?' I asked. 'Maybe the view I have of the world is a negative one. I would like to keep working on that tomorrow.' He said. When you change your view of the world, you will change the way you present. It wasn't even the same guy the next day! This was not just training but personal development."

Principle #5 from *How to Win Friends and Influence People*, in the category of *Be a Friendlier Person* is pretty simple: "Smile."

Visuals and Graphics

It's a good idea to make these points in a graphic form. Powerpoint has become the standard method, but unless we can use it well a flip chart is just as good. Many audiences will turn off at the sight of yet another PowerPoint presentation, because most of them are done poorly. Over 400 million desktops currently have the application—so if we want to stand out, we can't be like everyone else. We can use slides in our knockout presentations to highlight and emphasize key points. We should not rely on our slide projector to run the show or to provide our script.

We know of trainers who've had their computers crash or be stolen right before a presentation, had bulbs burn out mid-way, or been presenting when the entire city block lost power. They never missed a beat because they didn't rely on their slides. One sales person even completed her sales pitch in a rainy parking lot because the fire alarm went off in the middle of her presentation. She made the sale!

Pros and Cons of Bullet Points

Crafting a presentation when we're limited to bulleted concepts can be difficult. Instead, we should try writing out the story we would like to tell through our presentation. By formally capturing our thoughts in a written document, we can craft our story faster and easier.

Although a story isn't compelling if it doesn't flow properly, determining the best narrative can be difficult until all the parts have been recorded. Even best-selling authors rarely establish the flow without many rounds of reorganizing. So, after we've created our first draft and walked through a practice run, shift the content around until the flow feels natural and the presentation tells a compelling story. If we've backed up our key points with persuasive supporting content, such as industry statistics, analyst quotes, or customer testimonials, we're likely to see a positive response to our presentation. For better or for worse, bulleted lists tend to be the dominant form factor in PowerPoint. The advantage of bullet points is that they prevent overzealous authors from trying to convey every bit of information about our company and creating a slide overwhelmed by words. Bulleted lists present a concise summary of our message, and can be easily read by those listening to us. Our rule is to have no more than six words per bullet point, and no more than six bullet points per slide.

Then, we expand on points where necessary by speaking to them, which can often only be determined by "reading" the audience. To ensure that the bullet points are absorbed by the audience, make sure our bullets convey valuable information and are not reduced to industry jargon and sound bytes.

In a similar way, don't try to fit every piece of information about a point onto the slide. Leaving something for the speaker's notes ensures that the audience will listen to us and keeps the amount of screen-cluttering text to a minimum.

At the same time, our content should be memorable and meaningful to the prospect. Remember that people grasp pictures more quickly than words. Visually illustrate our points whenever possible with a graph or image and make sure we choose visuals that help to further the audience's comprehension of our points. For example, if we are trying to convey the idea that something has "high performance," an image of a Ferrari would instantly transmit that idea.

Let's introduce a small number of key phrases into our presentation to get our message across in the fewest possible words. They should include only essential information. Let's choose only the top points about our message and use these phrases to reference them consistently throughout the delivery. We should simplify and limit the number of words as much as we can.

Avoid using fancy fonts. Choose a font that is simple and comfortable for the audience to read such as Helvetica or Arial. At the most, use two different fonts. Keep the fonts large enough so that people at the back of the conference room will be able to see clearly what's on the screen.

Make the color of the text contrast with the background. Dark text on a light background is best in a bright room and light text on a dark background is best in a dark room. Patterned or textured backgrounds would reduce the readability of text. Keep the color scheme consistent throughout the presentation.

We may not be able to test our slides in the room before our presentation, but we can go to the far side of the room and see if we can read slides on our computer monitor.

Let's use templates carefully and effectively. When using a template, choose one that is appropriate for the content. A simple, straightforward layout is best if we are presenting to business clientele. Also, limit the number of slides. Don't try to insert too many slides, make sure that the presentation will not become too long. It also avoids the problem of continually changing slides during a business presentation. On average, one slide per minute is right, unless it's overwhelmed with charts, graphics and/or text. When we practice our presentation, we'll find out how many slides we need given the time allotted. Let's not be the person who zooms through twenty slides in the last minute because we never practiced.

Embedding photos, charts, graphs and even digitized videos will add variety and keep the audience interested in the presentation. Avoid using only text in the slides. And avoid cluttering the presentation with cute transitions and animations. Too many of them can distract our audience from what we are saying. Let's avoid doing anything in our slides that don't specifically relate to our message. A transition that zooms across the slide may be appropriate to convey the fact that things are moving rapidly in the business. Otherwise, why are we having slides zooming across the screen? "Because we can" is not a good answer.

We should definitely use visuals throughout the presentation. A picture really is worth a thousand words! Let's support our key ideas with an image whenever we can—one idea per image. Make it interesting, relevant, and powerful. And keep tracking the responses of the listeners throughout. Don't be afraid to ask for those responses directly. Use questions like these: "Can you see how this would be an improvement?" or "How would this help?" Interactive presentations keep listeners more involved and interested.

Visual Aids Lead to $500,000 Deposit

Paul Siregar, Managing Director for Dale Carnegie Indonesia, tells a story of how a quick thinking branch manager used visual aids in a client presentation. "A branch manager of the Indonesian operations of a European bank told me the following incident. The day before she had been at her office when one of her account managers asked her for help. Apparently her customers, a mother and her son, wanted to deposit some money and asked what the option with the best return was. This account manager then suggested putting the money in mutual funds. The customers were not sure what it was and the account manager had no idea how to persuade them so she ran to the branch manager asking for help. As it happened, the branch manager had just practiced presenting the concept of mutual funds using day-to-day items as an analogy during a High Impact Presentation session the day before, and the items were still in her car. So she went to her car, grabbed the exhibits, brought them to the conference room and proceeded to explain mutual funds using the same analogy she practiced. The customers were so convinced by her explanation that they deposited US$500,000."

Beyond Slides

PowerPoint slides are one way to convey information. Yet there are many other ways to convey information that can have as much or more impact! This chart illustrates the pros and cons of the various types of visual aids we might use in our presentations.

Video

Advantages	Disadvantages
• Professional quality, look, and image	• Expensive to produce
• Can be used with several different types of audiences	• Little or no audience participation
	• Impersonal presentation
• Does not require a facilitator for this part of the presentation	• Competes with the presenter
• Storage is easy	• Equipment may be complicated and expensive

Exhibits/Models

Advantages	Disadvantages
• Easier to understand • Can be attractive and eye catching • Can be very creative • Keep attention on the topic • Appeal to visual and kinesthetic learners	• Hard to keep looking fresh • Expensive • Can be difficult for everyone to see • Can distract from the message • Can compete with the presenter • Can be inflexible

Handouts

Advantages	Disadvantages
• Reduce the need for note taking • Provide some permanency for important information • Ensure that the information is accurately received	• Sometimes prompt premature questions • Transporting them is difficult • If poor quality, they reflect badly on the presenter • Can compete with the presenter

Wall Charts

Advantages	Disadvantages
• Can be very attractive • Influence the room environment • Give a consistent message • Make effective summaries • Reinforce the program message • Keep participants focused on message	• Difficult to maintain if transported • Not always convenient to hang • Can destroy the wall surface • Completely inflexible • Passive as far as audience involvement is concerned

Audio

Advantages	Disadvantages
• Gives variety to the presentation	• No visual aspect involved
• Can increase presenter's credibility	• Visual learners may not stay tuned in
• Adds value to listeners	• Presenter is marginalized
• Answers the question: "Who else says so besides you?"	• Requires additional equipment— quality is important
• Keeps listeners involved in presentation	• Can compete with presenter

Electronic Visuals

Advantages	Disadvantages
• High quality and professional look	• The room may need to be darkened when visuals are being used
• Creative; appeal to visual learners	• Can overpower the presenter
• Equipment is usually fairly reliable	• Sometimes hard for people to see
• Presentation consistency can be controlled	• Require laptop, data projector, and screen
• Easy and quick to customize	• Some experience is required to create

Smart Boards

Advantages	Disadvantages
• Can be very attractive	• Require technical installation with computer and hard wiring
• Influence the room environment	• Very difficult to move once installed
• Give a consistent message	• Relatively expensive
• Make effective summaries	• Can limit audience involvement.
• Reinforce the program message	• Handwriting must be clear, legible, and easy to read
• Keep participants focused on message	

Flip Charts

Advantages	Disadvantages
• The presenter maintains control	• Depend upon presenter's skill and style
• Created from information gathered from the audience	• Penmanship, writing, and spelling are important
• Portable	• Difficult to make copies for everyone
• Can be used by small groups	• Forty participants or fewer
• Don't burn out or crash	• Some stands are not easy to transport
	• Writing can put your back to the audience

White Boards

Advantages	Disadvantages
• Spontaneous	• Handwriting may be hard to read
• Semi-permanent	• Information is inconvenient to copy
• Identical information is provided to all	• Presenter's back may be turned to the audience for too long
• Provided constant view of information	• Limited to forty participants or fewer
• Keep audience involved in the presentation	• Writing can take a great deal of time

Jonathan Vehar recalls the time his father, Robert, a retired high school teacher, called him in a bit of a panic. Robert discovered that for teaching his evening community education class, he no longer had access to an overhead projector. "I guess I'll have to buy a laptop computer and put my slides in PowerPoint." Afraid that he'd end up being long-distance tech support for his non-computer savvy dad, Jonathan asked how many slides he had. "Six," said Robert. Jonathan then asked how many students were in the class. "It's a voice lesson class, so it's limited to six people." So Jonathan advised his father to have his slides blown up to poster-size and mounted on foam core. "Can I do that?!" his father asked? He can and he did! Jonathan then purchased his father a large portfolio case that would fit the posters to carry them to his classroom. His father put the posters in the chalk tray of the classroom, and reported that "they worked great!" Choosing the right visual aid format saved his father a lot of money on a laptop, time learning new technology, and Jonathan a lot of time providing technical support.

Handouts

If we're in person with a group, a supplement to using visual aids in a presentation is the use of handouts. (If we're working virtually, we can also send these along in advance.) When we give listeners something to take with them, it offers a way for them to remember and recall the material. Generally these are given before or during the presentation as a way to reinforce what we are saying.

Here are some of the benefits and challenges of using handouts, as well as some tips for using them.

Benefits
- Listeners take ownership, especially when they take notes
- Builds credibility of presenter

- Appeals to visual and kinesthetic learners
- Room for additional content, references, resources, etc.
- Provides a tangible, permanent resource for participants

Challenges

- Possible problems with printing, shipping, and transporting
- Uncertainty of how many copies to produce
- Can compete with your presentation
- People read forward, shuffle pages, look for inconsistencies

Key Tips

- Check in advance to determine if handouts are expected
- Check spelling, punctuation, and grammar for accuracy
- Determine best time to distribute: before, during, or after
- Announce if you intend to provide materials
- Adjust lighting levels so people can read and write
- Miniatures of electronic visuals are easiest to produce
- Print on both sides to show sensitivity to the environment
- Send electronic documents before or after the presentation
- If people ask for visuals, have them send you an email request
- Distribute when you are ready for people to read, not before
- Pre-count materials by rows or table groups to make distribution quicker

* * *

In this chapter, we've covered some of the important competencies when presenting. In the next chapter, we'll delve into one of the most important—and misused tools in presenting—telling stories.

Thoughts from a Master: Tina Graziotto, Vice President of Program Management and Instruction at Dale Carnegie Training of Western and Central Pennsylvania

If you had one piece of advice to share with someone who wants to be a better public speaker, what would it be?

My advice would be, first, you have to be clear about what your message is, if you're not clear you're going to fail.

Second is, practice out loud. Hear yourself saying the words. How it sounds in your head is not how it sounds to the audience.

From Dale Carnegie Himself

When you use exhibits, follow these suggestions and you will be assured of the rapt attention of your audience.

1. Keep the exhibit out of sight until you are ready to use it.
2. Use exhibits large enough to be seen from the very last row. Certainly your audience can't learn from any exhibit unless they see it.
3. Never pass an exhibit around among your listeners while you are speaking. Why invite competition?
4. When you show an exhibit, hold it up where your listeners can see it.
5. Remember, one exhibit that moves is worth ten that don't. Demonstrate if practicable.
6. Don't stare at the exhibit as you talk—you are trying to communicate with the audience, not with the exhibit.
7. When you have finished with the exhibit, get it out of sight if practicable.
8. If the exhibit you are going to use lends itself to "mystery treatment," have it placed on a table which will be at your side as you speak. Have it covered. As you talk, make references to it that will arouse curiosity—but don't tell what it is. Then, when you are ready to unveil it, you have aroused curiosity, suspense, and real interest.

Visual materials are becoming more and more prominent as devices to promote clarity. There is no better way to ensure that your audience will understand what you have to say than to go before them prepared to show as well as to tell them what you have in mind.

9: TELLING STORIES TO INSPIRE AUDIENCES TO ACTION

It was time for the big close. Mark Cahill had done his best with this talk and he knew it. He'd done his research and preparation, crafted a compelling opening statement, demonstrated how the technology worked so that the audience could see it in action, and now all that was left (other than a Question and Answer section at the end) was a strong close. He'd opened with a story and wanted to circle back to that same story to illustrate the value of selling the technology worldwide. "Earlier this afternoon, I shared with you a story about my grandfather. If he were alive today he would be amazed at the technology we're sharing. And yet, he would still . . ."

Woven throughout the chapters in this book were examples of how powerful authentic storytelling can be in a presentation. The art of telling an effective story isn't automatic, however. We've all heard people attempt to tell a story that didn't end well. They either rambled on and on with seemingly unrelated anecdotes or never got to the point.

The Most Important Part Of The Story

When thinking of stories, we may wonder, "What's the most important part of the story? Is it the opening? The close? Whether or not it was funny?" It's none of those. The most important part of the story is how it makes the audience feel.

> *"Remember that when dealing with human beings, we're creatures of emotion, not logic."*
> —DALE CARNEGIE

Poet, writer, and singer Maya Angelou once said, "People don't remember what you say, they remember how you make them feel." What this means is that when we are telling a story, we want to appeal to the audience both logically and emotionally. It's about focusing on the end result or action we want them to take and then showing them how to get there through a story.

The Magic Formula

Dale Carnegie has created a time-tested "Magic Formula" that provides the basic structure to build credibility, capture attention and call others to action. This formula will help us prepare effective communication that inspires others to act! Here's the Magic Formula for an effective story:

Incident + Action + Benefit

The *incident* is the heart of the story that helps set the scene, describes the action, and conveys the context for what comes next. The *action* is the action that we want our listeners to take; what we want them to do, think, or say. And the *benefit* is the value that they will realize when we take the action that we request.

Opening with a personal incident is one surefire way to grab favorable attention when we are trying to make a point. Relive a vivid, personal experience relevant to the point. This is what hooks people in and opens them up to persuasion. Listeners follow because we identify ourselves as part of a situation, and we want to know what is going to happen. No warm-up statements are needed. By launching directly into the incident, it's easier to capture an audience's attention. A speaker who begins with a personal story is secure with no loss of words or ideas.

Use Facts and Evidence. Facts, evidence, examples and stats support the statement of need for change. Start with a fact before explaining the message. Often an audience's minds are full of questions: Why should I listen, or why should I believe; who confirms that? Evidence is one of the primary tools we need to use when we want to convince someone of our views. This allows us to form a logical—not just emotional—response. Indicate what the evidence and the facts mean to you and what you believe. Use more real-life examples, analogies and testimonials.

Illustrate the Action. Effective persuasion requires us to simplify the message. Describe the story chronologically as it happened with all important clarifying details. Show that change was needed, and recommend a clear action for listeners to take in this situation.

Explain the Benefit. Connect the specific positive action to its benefit. All stories and anecdotes need to end with the benefit of the action we have taken or the problem we solved. This is a strong approach to optimize meaningful discussion and minimize emotional confrontations.

Every story we tell should follow this general formula to maximize its effectiveness.

Most magic formula stories are only 2–3 minutes. In our presentations to convey our point, we should be concise and strip out any extraneous detail. In our two minute story, figure that the first one minute and fifty seconds is the incident, the action is five seconds, and the benefit should take us five seconds.

Here's an example:

Incident: In 1996 when I was just starting out as a trainer, I received conflicting feedback in the course evaluations, and lower scores that I wanted. The evaluations showed that some people said that they appreciated my humor, but others said I was too stern. How could this be? I used a video camera to record one of my programs and I noticed that when I was thinking about what I was saying (which I did quite often because I was new to training and the content), I furrowed my brow. This made me look stern and angry. So even though I was saying things that were funny, I looked mad about it. No wonder people were confused! Once I saw what I was doing, and then confirmed it with a master trainer, I made a conscious effort to raise my eyebrows when I was speaking, and smiling while I was making a funny remark. Wow! What a difference in the course evaluations! The average overall rating increased substantially.

Action: So when you're talking in front of a group, and especially if you're saying something funny, use Dale Carnegie's Principle #5 from *How to Win Friends and Influence People*, and make sure you're in your happy place: Smile!

Benefit: People will enjoy your presentation, and you'll find that your evaluations can't help but improve.

Relive The Story, Don't Retell It

Dave Wright, CEO of Dale Carnegie Training Houston, Austin, San Antonio shares this advice for telling stories without getting lost in the emotion of them.

> "It's important to strike the right balance between logic and emotion. You want to walk along the shore. If it's too far away your story is dry, but if it's too far in the water you drown in emotion. If you do get too emotionally engaged, start to ask, 'What did you do next, what happened after that?' That will help you bring back in the logic to balance the emotion. If it's not emotionally engaging though, then ask, 'Why does this story matter?'

"For example, I coached a senior vice president of a research and development firm. Their general counsel had reached out to me. 'What's the issue?' I asked. 'I gave a presentation but was like Spock from Star Trek. Bland and emotionless. Apparently I need to add some life to my speaking.'

"Turns out he was totally inside of his head, thinking about himself and his presentation. So we did all kinds of wild and crazy drills to get him outside of his head. I had him tell a story like a circus barker. Then, we looked at the content of his story and made it a story from the heart. To help him, I asked him, 'How does this matter to you?'

"Then, we brought in several interns and he practiced his stories on them. They were impressed! The key is to relive the story—don't retell it. Come alive and bring your audience with you."

Dave shares some other sage advice when it comes to storytelling. "Also use different modalities and every part of their brain so they don't fall asleep. Change up the pace. Don't rely too much on visuals like slides. A guy called me a week before I was giving a presentation for his nonprofit, and he asked me to send my slide deck in advance. When he got them he plugged them in and started laughing. 'You only have three slides, and one's a picture.' It was true. When you practice enough, storytelling becomes natural."

Talk Like You're Talking To Your Friends

Robert Korp, Director of Training Quality EMEA for Dale Carnegie shares an anecdote about a person he was coaching who shifted his way of speaking to become more effective. "A person in a manufacturing company—a packaging producer—was a team lead and had gone through leadership training. He went back to the workplace and was presenting the information to the team, but he spoke in formal written-style language. I coached him by saying, 'Be yourself! Talk like you're talking to your friends.' He changed and exploded in a positive way. He was different and natural and convincing, because he was talking to his friends, not reciting a memo."

This is not to say "be overly informal." We want to avoid using colloquial terms, swearing, and telling off color stories. Being authentic and natural takes practice, but can absolutely be learned.

Mark Fitzmaurice, Director and Master Trainer, Dale Carnegie UK says, "When we use The Storytelling Formula we want to grab their attention straightaway. We live in a sound byte economy. We have seconds to grab their attention and keep it. The art of getting your message across is not putting too much wrapping paper or bubble wrap and getting to the message. We only have half as much time and twice as much information. The simplicity of the message is key."

There's now an entire industry around the art of storytelling and it was all started by Dale Carnegie in 1912! It's how history worked before books.

The Keys to Effective Storytelling

- Establish "Who," "What," "When," "Where," "How," and "Why."
- Include animation and vocal variety.
- Narrow the "Action" and broaden the "Benefit."
- Use Analogies
- Back it up with evidence in the form of a personal anecdote or story
- When using The Magic Formula
    —Get into the incident right away
    —Get to the heart, not the filler/wrapper
    —Be concise
- When communicating with the audience do the following
    —Use their name when possible
    —Thank them for their contribution
    —Customize the delivery to listeners and that specific audience

Thoughts from a Master: Ken Beyersdorf, President, Dale Carnegie of Arizona

If you had one piece of advice to share with someone who wants to be a better public speaker, what would it be?

"When you look at individuals who want to become effective public speakers, I always tell people, You want to become very natural. Don't be 'Presentation Ken' and then 'Regular Ken.' Presentation Ken means you are trying too hard to project something that you think others want you to be. It comes down to congruency. If I hear your tone and how you speak and if it's different on stage, I'm not going to trust you. Don't try and memorize your talk. In a one-on-one conversation you don't usually forget, but when we are giving a presentation we can forget because our eyes and our mind are not focused on what we are saying. Remember that you are speaking to one person. Whether it's five people or a thousand, it's one person. They are different individuals. You don't forget what you're saying and you come across more natural and relaxed."

From Dale Carnegie Himself

Suppose you want to give an illustration of how you succeeded in calming down an irate customer by using one of the rules of human relations. You could begin like this: "The other day a man came into my office. He was pretty mad because the appliance we had sent out to his house only the week before was not working properly. I told him that we would do all we could to remedy the situation. After a while he calmed down and seemed satisfied that we had every intention to make things right." This anecdote has one virtue—it is fairly specific—but it lacks names, specific details, and, above all, the actual dialogue which would make this incident come alive.

Here it is with these added qualities: "Last Tuesday, the door of my office slammed and I looked up to see the angry features of Charles Blexam, one of my regular customers. I didn't have time to ask him to take a seat. 'Kid, this is the last straw,' he said, 'you can send a truck right out and cart that wash machine out of my basement.' I asked him what was up. He was too willing to reply. 'It won't work,' he shouted, 'the clothes get all tangled, and my wife's sick and tired of it.' I asked him to sit down and explain it in more detail. 'I haven't got time to sit down. I'm late for work and I wish I'd never come in here to buy an appliance in the first place. Believe me, I'll never do it again.' Here he hit the desk with his hand and knocked over my wife's picture. 'Look, Charley,' I said, 'if you will just sit down and tell me all about it, I promise to do whatever you want me to do.' With that, he sat down, and we calmly talked it over."

It isn't always possible to work dialogue into your talk, but you can see how the direct quotation of the conversation in the excerpt above helps to dramatize the incident for the listener. If the speaker has some imitative skill and can get the original tone of voice into the words, dialogue can become more effective. Also, dialogue gives your speech the authentic ring of everyday conversation. It makes you sound like a real person talking across a dinner table, not like a pedant delivering a paper before a learned society or an orator ranting into a microphone.

10: GRACE UNDER PRESSURE

". . . And this story powerfully illustrates why expanding the sales of the technology so that our global customers can reap the benefits is so important. In the words of our vision statement . . . if not now, when?" Mark Cahill watched as everyone in the conference room smiled, nodded, and softly clapped. Everyone except one person. The CFO, Gordon Rickman, sat stone-faced with his arms crossed. He appeared to be glaring! Mark's heart sank because he was about to launch into the Q and A session. Gordon was notorious for asking hostile questions and getting extremely defensive when questioned. "It's actually a miracle he waited and let me finish," Mark thought. Taking a deep breath, he asked the words he didn't want to say. "Who has the first question?"

There's an old adage that says, "If anything can go wrong, it will go wrong." This chapter is designed to help us anticipate and avoid the issues and problems that can happen when presenting. From stage fright to technical problems, trust us when we say that even when things go wrong, all is not lost. The main thing to remember is, "Don't panic." Do your best to smile, laugh, and handle whatever the problem is with grace.

Stage Fright Is Common

There are stories of entertainment superstars who undergo extraordinary episodes of stage fright immediately before they appear in public. They experienced blurred vision, nausea, and headaches—even after performing hundreds of times. If these professionals face so much anxiety on stage, it's no wonder that we may all be fearful of appearing before a group—especially when our financial well-being depends on it. That anxiety may even cause us to avoid speaking opportunities altogether, which can have a seriously negative effect on our careers.

There are lots of relaxation methods that can help reduce fear of presenting to a group, but the most important step is recognizing what the situation really calls for. Making presentations is a learned skill. For most of us, it is not something we can just get up and do without some basic training.

Ken Beyersdorf, President of Dale Carnegie of Arizona, shares a story about stage fright. "There was a gentleman taking a class on self-confidence, standing up front with five other people. He was terrified! The task was to give a simple introduction and he was gripping the table in the front of the room so tightly you could see his knuckles turning white. 'What am I supposed to say?' he asked. We had to walk him through it one question at a time. It was really stage fright at its worst. It was a twelve week program and in the final week we asked participants, 'What is the greatest benefit you received from the program?' His answer? 'Self-confidence.' Ironically, as he was giving his final presentation the poster on the wall behind him fell on the ground and he literally just turned around and put it back on the wall, not missing a beat of his presentation. He didn't forget what he was saying, get flustered, or anything. He spoke for two and a half minutes."

Practice Reduces Anxiety

Rehearsing our presentations over and over again will greatly reduce anxiety. The more familiar we become with our material, the more passionate and convincing our presentations will become. The more comfortable we feel with our words, the more natural our speech will sound. That's why the best pros practice again and again.

Video and audio recordings are two very simple ways to rehearse our presentations. Video obviously will give the most complete picture, and nothing will improve our presentations more than seeing ourselves on tape. We'll notice mannerisms that maybe we didn't expect to see. As much as we may not want to watch ourselves, it is a powerful learning experience. And it's as simple as picking up our phones and tapping a few buttons. Then, "Action!"

Digital recording apps on our phones are easy to use almost anywhere, and we can even listen to our presentations in the car. When we hear ourselves, we know right away if we're speaking too quickly, too slowly, or if some words are difficult to pronounce. We hear every mistake in grammar and all the "um's" and "ah's." Listening to all our mistakes can be hard, but at least we're the only ones that hear them. By the time we get to the presentation, we'll have corrected them.

Questions and Answers

One of the most nerve wracking parts of any talk can be the Question and Answer section. Why? Because it's the one part of the presentation that we can't fully practice. Despite this, there are quite a few benefits to having a Q&A session at the end of our talks. There are some risks as well.

Benefits of Question and Answer Sessions
- Clarifies the message
- Reinforces the key points
- Gets resistance out in the open
- Offers opportunities to add more evidence and examples
- Encourages audience interaction

Challenges and Risks
- Some questions are difficult to answer
- One audience member may dominate the discussion
- Time constraints may be hard to enforce

- Some audiences are non-responsive
- Some audiences are hostile

Handling Q&A Issues

How can we minimize the risks and challenges with the question and answer session? Here are some suggestions.

Set Time Limits

Communicate clearly, in the beginning, how much time will be allotted for the question-and-answer period. This helps keep the questions and answers short and to the point. The general guideline is to keep answers short. The short answer allows for more questions. On occasion, it is advantageous to take the liberty of a longer answer, particularly if there was not enough time to develop that point in the presentation. Be sure someone from the audience does not use the questioning privilege to make a speech. If that begins to happen, gracefully force the person to ask a question. It is also important not to let any one person dominate the questioning period. It is our responsibility to remain in control. If we do not know the answer to a specific question, say so. Honesty gains respect and demonstrates that we are credible. When we try to bluff our way through the answer, we lose credibility. People can tell when we're bluffing.

Open the Question & Answer Period

Applause generally follows immediately after a presentation; then, it is simply a matter of saying, "I have _____ minutes for questions and answers. Who has the first question?" Our request says that we expect questions, and now is the time for the first one. An expectant look on our face and raising our hand shows the audience what to do next. Be sure to give time for the group to politely figure out who will go first. Count to ten before deciding no one has a question.

Look At The Person Asking The Question.

Stay focused and demonstrate good listening skills. Maintain a pleasant facial expression and welcome the question. Once we have heard and understood the question, turn to the rest of the audience,and paraphrase the question. By paraphrasing, we gain some time to gather our thoughts and make sure everyone else has heard the question. Probably most important, however, is that we remain in control and make it "our" question. Restatement of the question also gives us an opportunity to take the "sting" or the "barb" out of the question, if that was the intention of a hostile member of the audience. If the question was, "Your team is always missing your targets and overspending on budgets and it makes the rest of us look bad. When are you finally going to do something about it?" We can paraphrase it as, "The question is about targets and budgets. It is true that we have run up against some unforeseen challenges in our development . . ." This reframe allows us to answer the question without getting defensive or adding fuel to the antagonism.

When No One Has a Question, Ask One Yourself

Sometimes, after a presenter asks for questions, the audience does not respond. Most often, this simply means that our listeners are unsure of how "safe" it is to ask questions. After counting to ten, we might ask a question ourselves to stimulate the audience. For instance, we could say: "A question often asked is . . ." and then answer the question. Then ask, "Who has the next question?" This usually sets the stage for further questions. Don't be overly afraid of a few seconds of silence. The audience wants to fill that silence as much as we do. If, however, the audience still remains silent after another ten count, ask another question and answer it. Twice is enough. Thank the audience for their attention, and then we give our second prepared closing.

Close the Question & Answer Period

When we know our time is about to run out, ask, "Who has the final question?" This signals the audience that answering questions is about to come to an end. When we have answered the final question, gracefully thank the audience for their interest, and we give our . . .

Second prepared closing

We have two opportunities to close our presentations with a call to action, and we should prepare both of them. We have one closing at the end of our formal remarks where we should ask people to do something specific, and then we have another opportunity to make a similar request of the audience at the close of the Q&A. We shouldn't miss either opportunity! Just because we ask once doesn't mean our job is done. We will need to keep asking until our audience takes action accordingly.

Technical Issues

Sometimes, despite our best efforts to plan and prepare, things go wrong. Our mechanical equipment fails, there's a problem with the room, the lighting, the air conditioning or heating system, a crucial piece of equipment stops working, et cetera. Here is a chart that can help us anticipate and prevent some of the most common problems.

Presentation Support Tools: Options and Tips		
Video	**Wall Charts**	**Smart Boards**
• Test equipment prior to use • Dim but do not darken room • Use video with appropriate discussion questions • The video should be less than ten minutes in length • It shouldn't be the presentation	• Protect the charts to keep them looking new • Use them to introduce a topic, summary or transition • Display continually for convenient reference • Be careful not to damage walls	• Make writing neat and large for easy information capture • Need special markers and eraser • Keep batteries charged • Capture all the ideas before erasing • Face audience when speaking

Exhibits/Models	Audio	Flip Charts
• Place exhibit where all can see • Remove it when finished with it • Do not talk while the exhibit is being examined • Face the audience not the exhibit • It should enhance the presentation, not compete with the speaker	• Production quality is important • Make it short enough to keep audience attention • Allow appropriate discussion time afterwards • Remember, audio provides no body language to enhance impact	• Gather discussion information and make it visible • Provide a variety of colored markers that work • Post pages when appropriate • Provide a chart to each group • Penmanship is important
Handouts	**Electronic Visuals**	**White Boards**
• Have extras available • Organize or bind professionally • Distribute before or after talk so they don't compete with you • Make sure contact information is on the handouts if you wish to be contacted	• Combine text and graphics • Don't darken room too much • Ensure you have a back-up set • Ensure projector is available • Always face the audience • Allow set up and practice time • Black slide during presentation	• Print large enough for everyone to see • Good to use for brainstorming or group planning • Keep fresh markers available • Clean the surface immediately after each use

Bring An "Emergency Kit"

One way for us to stay calm when things go wrong is to do our best to anticipate what might happen and then bring a backup. Here is a short list of some items that our trainers bring with them to presentations.

- Throat lozenges
- Painkillers in case of a headache
- Allergy medicine and tissues
- Spare toothbrush and toothpaste for after lunch presentations
- A bottle of water
- A remote control device to change slides
- Batteries for any wireless technology
- A USB with your presentation backed up on it
- Paper copy of any notes, even if you're planning on using slides
- Spare chargers for your phone, laptop, and any other electronic devices
- A change of clothes in case of a spill
- An energy bar or small portable snack
- A spare copy of our introduction printed out for the introducer
- Flip chart markers and masking tape
- Adapters for common projector plugs that work with your laptop's input plugs (e.g. HDMI into USB-C)

In this chapter, we've covered how to handle some of the common things that can go wrong in a presentation. As we've mentioned throughout this chapter, the most important thing to remember when something goes wrong is to not panic! Technical problems won't derail our credibility with the audience unless we let them.

"If you're not nervous, you should probably sit down."
NANCY COVERT, PRESIDENT OF DALE CARNEGIE
OF BIRMINGHAM AND HUNTSVILLE, AL

Thoughts from a Master: Frank Starkey, Vice President of Training and Master Trainer at Dale Carnegie Training of Dallas and Fort Worth

If you had one piece of advice to share with someone who wants to be a better public speaker, what would it be?

I have been around the Dale Carnegie organization since 1988, and am once again re-reading *How To Win Friends and Influence People.* The bottom line when it comes to speaking is that it's not about me, it's about the other person. The shortest distance between two people is a great story. It's the most powerful way to connect with another person. Not going "me me me" or being in "presentation mode" but telling a story to appeal emotionally as well as logically. Whatever the outcome is, it comes back to how we connect with other people.

From Dale Carnegie Himself

Is it not evident that the speaker who argues with his audience is merely arousing their stubbornness, putting them on the defensive, making it well-nigh impossible for them to change their minds? Is it wise to start by saying, "I am going to prove so and so?" Aren't your hearers liable to accept that as a challenge and remark silently, "Let's see you do it?"

Is it not much more advantageous to begin by stressing something that you and all of your hearers believe, and then to raise some pertinent question that everyone would like to have answered? Then take your audience with you in an earnest search for the answer.

While on that search, present the facts as you see them so clearly that they will be led to accept your conclusions as their own. They will have much more faith in some truth that they have discovered for themselves.

"The best argument is that which seems merely an explanation." In every controversy, no matter how wide and bitter the differences, there is always some common ground of agreement on which a speaker can invite everyone to meet.

Contradicting ideas are much less likely to arise in the listener's mind when the speaker presents his ideas with feeling and contagious enthusiasm. I say "contagious," for enthusiasm is just that. It thrusts aside all negative and opposing ideas. When your aim is to convince, remember it is more productive to stir emotions than to arouse thoughts. Feelings are more powerful than cold ideas. To arouse feelings one must be intensely in earnest. Regardless of the petty phrases a man may concoct, regardless of the illustrations he may assemble, regardless of the harmony of his voice and the grace of his gestures, if he does not speak sincerely, these are hollow and glittering trappings. If you would impress an audience, be impressed yourself. Your spirit, shining through your eyes, radiating through your voice, and proclaiming itself through your manner, will communicate itself to your audience.

Every time you speak, and especially when your avowed purpose is to convince, what you do determines the attitude of your listeners. If you are lukewarm, so will they be; if you are flippant and antagonistic, so will they be.

11: SPEAKING VIRTUALLY

"We just have a few questions, Mark. I appreciate you willing to speak to us remotely like this."

Mark Cahill had just arrived home from his presentation to the executive team when he'd gotten word that a few of the investors had some additional questions. He'd be asked to talk with them over Zoom.

"No problem! What can I help you with?"

Everything Has Changed, But Most Things Stayed The Same

No book on presentations and public speaking would be complete without a chapter that addresses the challenges of presenting virtually. Our company, like millions of others around the world, could very well have come to a standstill when our in-person training and talks had to stop due to the Covid-19 pandemic. Fortunately, with the ideas you'll discover in this chapter, we were quickly able to pivot to online training based on years of working with clients, meeting internally, and delivering clients in a live online format.

These days, virtual meetings and presentations are the norm rather than the exception. While most of what we've covered in this book apply to both in-person and virtual presentations, there are some important ways we need to adjust our approach to maximize the online medium.

With in-person meetings, the audience is right there in front of you. The participants can't turn off their camera or pretend to pay attention. They can't put up an image of themselves in the chair and leave to go get some coffee, or easily check their email while still staring at the screen as some people do in online meetings.

Virtually, we have to compete with home and work distractions, conflicting priorities and diminished attention spans. We have to work harder to keep the audience engaged.

Mark Fitzmaurice, Director and Master Trainer, Dale Carnegie UK says, "In person, a lot of communication happens subliminally. The challenge online is that's missing. We don't have subliminal messaging but only have voice and body language to use. What happens is that a lot of presenters don't make any changes and that can fall flat. You have to work harder at modulating your voice. You can't just do what you did when you were in person. You have to work a little harder."

Conveying Body Language Online

What does it mean to "work a little harder?" It means that we have to consciously think about how we are going to convey body language online. We don't have the ability to walk around the room as we would in person. We can still convey passion and congruence with the rest of our body.

Mark Fitzmaurice goes on to say, "We want congruence. We want them to feel what we are saying. With body language (even online) you can convey passion. What do you do with your hands? Do you stand up? Speak with the whole of your body. Make sure your body language and voice are congruent with your message."

> *"We are professionals. Take care of how you look, what's going on behind you, etc. Take care of your image. Even when you are presenting online 'Go to work.'"*
> —MARK FITZMAURICE, DIRECTOR AND MASTER TRAINER, DALE CARNEGIE UK

Twenty Tips For Getting It Right

Here are some tips and techniques for success in your virtual presentations.

1. Look at the camera. When we are presenting online, we want to make sure we are looking at the camera, not

just the screen. This means literally looking at the red or green dot on the camera as if it were the audience. Put the camera at eye level so you aren't looking up at it. If you're looking down at the camera, you risk getting a double chin or some other unflattering image. Get close to the camera but not so close that your image is far larger than everyone else's. People are drawn naturally to look at faces, and maintaining a natural distance can help that.

2. Pay attention to your background. Most of us have seen the "behind the scenes" images of newscasters who presented the nightly news from their homes. The camera would look at an office or a green screen, and the rest of the room might be a spare bedroom or basement. Avoid clutter or overly personal items such as family photos or a bookshelf. Your audience will be looking at your library and pictures instead of listening to you. If you don't have a good background, most online presentation platforms allow you to upload a background from your computer to use as a virtual background or will allow you to blur your background. At Dale Carnegie Training we have several corporate backgrounds to choose from. It can be a good opportunity to market your brand by having a logo or your company name behind you as you present.

3. Don't rely on ambient lighting. Make sure you have a good front light, where the light shines brightly on

your face. If there is a window to your back or one side, close the shades or curtains to avoid glare or a backlight that darkens your face. Natural light can be flattering, but is unpredictable. If you plan to do a lot of virtual presentations, consider investing in a ring light.

4. Master your technology before the presentation. Nothing can destroy our credibility faster than if we are fumbling around with unfamiliar technology. In fact, if you can have someone there to help you run the technology, you can focus on conveying the message. Either way, have a "dress rehearsal" of your entire talk with the same technical setup (internet connection and computer) as you'll have the day of the talk.

5. Be aware of when your camera and microphone are on. We have all seen embarrassing footage from people who thought their cameras or microphones were off and said or did something humiliating. Always assume it is on, and you're less likely to embarrass yourself. If you are part of a panel or a group presentation, look at the camera and pay attention even when you aren't speaking! High impact speakers understand the importance of making eye contact—especially online.

6. Consider standing up. One way to effectively use body language is to stand up while presenting. This can be a challenge if you are using a virtual background but can help create the same energy as an in-person

presentation. Be sure to place the camera at eye level so the camera—and your audience—isn't looking up at you.

7. Lean forward. If you have to sit, sit up tall with your rear end to the back of the chair and lean forward. This sends the message that you are actively engaged with the audience. This is especially critical if someone else is speaking.

8. Watch your tone. Because the audience doesn't have the benefit of you moving around the stage, one way to keep them engaged is through an animated vocal tone. Don't speak too softly or with a monotone voice. Conversely, don't become so animated that your energy drains the audience.

9. Testing 1,2,3. Be sure and test out your microphone beforehand. If your audience can't hear you, your message can't get through. Also test your headphones or computer speaker to make sure there is no interference or distortion. Again, if you intend to do a lot of virtual presentations, consider investing in a higher quality microphone and/or headset.

10. Pace yourself. Speaking too slowly or quickly can detract from your presentation as well. Many times our nerves can get the best of us and we start to speak quickly. Slow it down!

11. Plug into your modem. If possible, plug your computer directly into your modem using an ethernet cable. Doing so will give you the strongest possible internet connection so that you aren't risking a weak or unstable connection in the middle of your presentation as a result of the vagaries of wi-fi.

12. Have a backup. Just as with in-person presentations, have a backup of your slides or visual aids. Also make sure that someone else (somewhere else) has a copy so that if your internet crashes and you have to call in your presentation over the phone, the audience will still be able to see the visual aids. Even better? Have a backup plan to your backup plan.

13. Be sure and use visual images. It's even more important in virtual presentations that we use visual aids. The audience needs something to look at in order to stay engaged. However, the same advice applies to creating your slides. Keep them simple and limit the amount of text on each slide. Don't leave the same slide up for too long. Keep them moving, or take them off of the screen until you're ready for the next one.

14. Don't chat. One distinctive feature of virtual presentations is the ability of participants to ask questions and comment through the chat. It's a great way to keep the audience engaged, but be sure to have someone else running that part of the presentation.

It's far too easy to get distracted and start thinking about commenting on what you're reading in the chat or saying hello to the participants. If you ask people to answer a question or comment on something, pause your talking and read them aloud or comment on them. Make it a planned part of the talk, and only refer to the chats at that time.

15. Interact with the audience. Just because we are virtual doesn't mean that we cannot engage the audience. Just as if you were doing an in-person presentation, incorporate audience engagement. You can use chats, polls, and raised hands. Don't go for more than about ten minutes without some form of audience participation. If you plan to use breakout rooms, go in each of them and interact there.

16. Use their names:. Dale Carnegie said that "a person's name is to that person the sweetest and most important sound in any language." Use your participant list and interact with them by name. Have them raise their hands if they want to speak.

17. Mute the audience. Set the default settings to "mute" for the audience microphones until you are ready for group interaction. Hearing a dog barking or papers shuffling can be very distracting!

18. Be yourself. The advice we give for in-person presentations is the same with virtual ones. Be your authentic

self. Don't try and put on a show or be someone you're not. Let your personality shine through! People will remember the information better if they feel you are sincere.

19. Keep the audience in mind. Remember, it's not about you. It's about the audience. Stay focused on your message and making sure that everyone is staying engaged and interacting.

20. Monday Morning Quarterback. In sports, after a game, the coach takes the players into the locker room and shows video footage of the various plays from the game so that the players can analyze areas for improvement. If possible, record your talk and watch it later. See where you can improve and what you did well. Presenting is about continually getting better, and that comes from evaluating your performance.

Thoughts from a Master: Mark Fitzmaurice, Director and Master Trainer, Dale Carnegie UK

If you had one piece of advice to share with someone who wants to be a better public speaker, what would it be?

I grew up on a council estate on the poor end of town. I was one of seven children under the age of ten. My home life was literally like a zoo and it made me very insecure. Who would listen to me when there was always someone else there who was louder and more demanding?

When I was twenty six, my company put me on a Dale Carnegie course. It was a management course and we were broken into small groups. I had to stand up and give a presentation and I had never been more scared in my entire life. Why? Because I was focused on me.

During the course of the training, I learned that it wasn't about me. It was about my message. By the end of the training, they voted me best of the table.

This was thirty four years ago and I still remember the names of the other two people at my table. There was a millionaire and a business magnate, and I won. That moment changed my life.

Later, I went to a fourteen week speaking training class and for the first six weeks I couldn't look at the audience. I looked out the window. Finally, in the sixth week, I talked about something important to me (a promotion at work) and I looked at the audience. I won, and got a pen as an award. I still have that pen. I now train people all over the world. The truth is, anybody can be brilliant.

As a speaker, you have to be able to transmit your emotions. Sometimes it's enthusiasm and sometimes it's softness. This requires you to be in touch with your own emotions and have the courage to show your own vulnerability. Put yourself on show, you give people a sense of who you are. Don't be a guest in your own life.

Learning this can change your life!

From Dale Carnegie Himself

Get the Facts About
The Fear of Speaking In Public

Fact Number One: You are not unique in your fear of speaking in public. Surveys in colleges indicate that eighty to ninety per cent of all students enrolled in speech classes suffer from stage fright at the beginning of the course. I am inclined to believe that the figure is higher among adults at the start of my course, almost one hundred per cent.

Fact Number Two: A certain amount of stage fright is useful! It is nature's way of preparing us to meet unusual challenges in our environment. So, when you notice your pulse beating faster and your respiration speeding up, don't become alarmed. Your body, ever alert to external stimuli, is getting ready to go into action. If these physiological preparations are held within limits, you will be capable of thinking faster, talking more fluently, and generally speaking with greater intensity than under normal circumstances.

Fact Number Three: Many professional speakers have assured me that they never completely lose all stage fright. It is almost always present just before they speak, and it may persist through the first few sentences of their talk.

This is the price these men and women pay for being like race horses and not like draft horses. Speakers who say they are "cool as a cucumber" at all times are usually as thick-skinned as a cucumber and about as inspiring as a cucumber.

Fact Number Four: The chief cause of your fear of public speaking is simply that you are unaccustomed to speaking in public. "Fear is misbegotten of ignorance and uncertainty," says Professor Robinson in *The Mind in the Making.* For most people, public speaking is an unknown quantity, and consequently one fraught with anxiety and fear factors. For the beginner, it is a complex series of strange situations, more involved than, say, learning to play tennis or drive a car. To make this fearful situation simple and easy: practice, practice, practice. You will find, as thousands upon thousands have, that public speaking can be made a joy instead of an agony merely by getting a record of successful speaking experiences behind you.

How well you succeed is largely determined by thoughts you have prior to speaking. See yourself in your imagination talking to others with perfect self control.

It is easily in your power to do this. Believe that you will succeed. Believe it firmly, and you will then do what is necessary to bring success about.

CONCLUSION

It had been a week since Mark Cahill had given his presentation to the executive team and he was awaiting their decision. After some tense questions from the CFO about how much the technology expansion would cost, the team thanked him and told him they would contact him in a few days.

"Mark, it's in." Mark's personal assistant had been monitoring the e-mail address and was told to notify him as soon as the message from headquarters came in. Mark was a little nervous as he clicked open the email, but he felt confident that the presentation had gone as well as it possibly could have. "Here goes . . ." he thought as he began to read.

"On behalf of the entire executive team, I want to thank you for coming in earlier this week to present your ideas on the tech expansion. You made a strong case and brought up some great ideas. We talked about it as a team and are pleased to say that we'll be going ahead with your proposal. I'll have my sec-

retary forward some documentation in the next couple of days. For now, just let me congratulate you and say 'Well done.'"

Throughout this book, we've read stories and tips from the people at Dale Carnegie Training who are in the field teaching and living this material every day. Through the process of learning to "overcome the fear and horror of public speaking" we find that we gain so much more than presentation competency. We become a better version of ourselves as people. It's about so much more than speaking better. It's about leading better. It's about changing the world for the better bit by bit. It's about BEING better.

Practice Compassion

As you are reading this material and practicing what you've learned, be kind to yourself. It takes time to get outside of your comfort zone, push past fear, and learn to bring the authentic person you are to the stage.

Use the principles Dale Carnegie taught on yourself! Begin with praise and honest appreciation. Focus on what's good and where you see growth. Observe progress that you're making up the hill. Not how far you still have to climb.

Some Final Advice From Our Experts

You can get the same level of engagement with online presentations as you can with in-person ones. These days, you can even fall in love online! Embrace the fact that effective presentations happen everywhere and anywhere. Online or in the hallway over coffee. The principles are the same.

—Dave Wright, CEO of Dale Carnegie Training
Houston, Austin and San Antonio

—⁓—

I remember a person from the board of a large pharmaceutical distributor. He was at the C-suite level. When he started the training he was very clear, "I hate presenting." But the High Impact Presentations training shows us how to use stories and be yourself. A couple of weeks later, this same person went from "I hate presenting" and it being a nasty duty, to being something he loved and was good at! The most important thing is not the rhetorical structure or organization of the presentation, but how people operate in their shells and how to get rid of them.

—Robert Korp, Director of Training Quality
EMEA for Dale Carnegie

—⁓—

The manager/engineer at a high security/expert company realized when he got promoted into management that he needed to work on the culture. The attitude at the time was, "We are the way we are and are okay. We aren't as good at challenging ourselves and showing who we are." So he sent the team through High Impact Presentations training. They spent two days focusing on how they could communicate better. We need to be more personal as managers to create a better atmosphere. We have to dare to be personal. Dare to communicate personally. We also need to be an attractive employer. We need to show transparency through personal stories. To attract a quality employee, you have to be able to present. Stories can do this.

There was also a consultant in another organization who felt that she was a little bullied and being treated poorly and not being included in things. Her manager was surprised, saying, "We have such a good environment here." The CEO realized they were talking about solving business issues and not developing each other. So they put everyone who was in the network that was going through the training into a chorus and they had singing practice once a week. You can imagine the first week was awkward, but they started to realize that they were good! Over time the culture of the group changed and the woman started being included. There is a power in doing something that no one is an expert at and then realize you can be good at it. Everyone starts at the same level and inclusion happens.

Learning to become a better presenter can have so many benefits, from improving the culture of the company to being a more attractive employer. And it all starts with being who we really are.

—Berit Friman, CEO of Dale Carnegie, Sweden

—⚊—

In April of 2020, everything was shutting down from the pandemic. One of the people who had gone through our training had come down with COVID-19 early on. People were dying left and right and this man said to his wife and child, "I just talked to my doctor and I am going into the hospital. You can't come with me, and I may never see you again. I love you."

He was in the hospital for nearly a week and had his Bible with him and a few other things. One of the things he brought were the 3 x 5 notecards that we give out in our training sessions where we teach honest and sincere appreciation. Everyone writes down something that they appreciate about that person. As he focused on surviving this life threatening disease, he kept reading those cards over and over again. He tells us that reading the words of value, acknowledgment and appreciation written about himself helped him survive. He left the hospital, went home to his wife and child, and healed.

If there is one thing to take away from Speak: How to Overcome the Fear and Horror of Public Speaking it's this: You have something valuable to say. You are worth listening to. Let that out and "be a good person, speaking." Your listeners need to hear what's inside. And this you do for them.

—Frank Starkey, Vice President of Training and Master Trainer at Dale Carnegie Training in Dallas and Fort Worth, TX

—⁓—

Don't be afraid to practice. Use your camera on the phone. It's a great way to overcome fear. It's a skill like anything else. Record yourself.

Also, with the Dale Carnegie principles, use them on yourself. It's important that we be kind to ourselves. You'll hate your first time on camera. Don't focus on what's wrong, focus on what's good and how much progress you're making. When you climb a mountain you only see how far you have to go. Remember to begin with praise and honest appreciation of yourself and don't criticize and complain.

—Mark Fitzmaurice, Director and Master Trainer,
Dale Carnegie UK

From Dale Carnegie Himself

When we learn any new thing, like French or golf or speaking in public, we never advance steadily. We do not improve gradually. We do it by waves, by abrupt starts and sudden stops. Then we remain stationary for a time, or we may even slip back and lose some of the ground we have previously gained. These periods of stagnation, or retrogression, are well known by all psychologists; they have been named "plateaus in the curve of learning." Students of effective speaking will sometimes be stalled, perhaps for weeks, on one of these plateaus. Work as hard as they may, they cannot seem to get off it. The weak ones give up in despair.

Those with grit persist, and they find that suddenly, almost overnight, without knowing how or why it has happened, they have made great progress. They have lifted from the plateau like an airplane. Abruptly they have acquired naturalness, force, and confidence in their speaking.

You may always, as has been stated elsewhere in these pages, experience some fleeting fear, some shock, some nervous anxiety, the first few moments you face an audience. Even the greatest musicians have felt it in spite of their innumerable public appearances. Paderewski always fidgeted nervously with his cuffs immediately before he sat down at the piano. But as soon as he began to play, all of his audience-fear vanished quickly like a mist in August sunshine.

His experience will be yours. If you will but persevere, you will soon eradicate everything, including this initial fear; and that will be initial fear, and nothing more. After the first few sentences, you will have control of yourself. You will be speaking with positive pleasure.

TOP PRESENTATION TIPS

1. Consider yourself honored by being asked to address an audience—and say so!
2. Give your listeners sincere appreciation.
3. Mention the names of some listeners.
4. Play yourself down—not up!
5. Say "we"—not "you."
6. Don't talk with "a scowling face and an upbraiding voice."
7. Talk in terms of your listeners' interests.
8. Have a good time delivering your talk.
9. Don't apologize.
10. Appeal to the nobler emotions of your audience.
11. Welcome criticism instead of resenting it.
12. Be "a good person skilled in speaking."

APPENDIX A:
Presentation Planning Worksheet

Presentation Planning Worksheet

Guidelines

- Project a positive attitude about our message
- Open and close with impact
- Determine the main points of our message
- Use energetic body language and an upbeat tone of voice
- Select positive illustrations that support our message

The Basic Structure of a Presentation

Opening: Favorably attract immediate interest from the audience.

Message: Clearly state the message or theme.

Evidence: Establish credibility and inspire respect and confidence by using convincing evidence.

Closing: Leave the audience with a favorable, memorable impression of you and your organization.

Preparation: Describe the audience and purpose of the presentation:

Outline

Opening:

_____

_____

_____

_____

_____

_____

_____

First fact, benefit, evidence:

_____

_____

_____

_____

_____

_____

_____

Second fact, benefit, evidence:

_____

_____

_____

_____

_____

_____

_____

Third fact, benefit, evidence:

_____

_____

_____

_____

_____

_____

_____

Closing:

_____

_____

_____

_____

_____

_____

_____

APPENDIX B:
Speak More Effectively
By Dale Carnegie

Effective communication is critical in any organization; the mark of a great communicator is the ability to energize a team, a boardroom, or an arena.

What does it take to be a great communicator? Being a subject matter expert alone doesn't guarantee a riveting presentation. Deep content knowledge may earn you the right to speak but conveying the excitement you have for your message is equally important—if not more so. If an audience senses your genuine passion for your topic, they will hang on every word. While they may appreciate your knowledge, it's your enthusiasm that will truly engage people.

To date, life has prepared you to make at least a dozen great speeches that no one else could deliver, because no one else has had precisely your experiences. Talking publicly about your own experiences should be no more difficult than telling a good story to a friend. We'll help you to develop the courage and self-confidence to speak clearly and concisely in any public setting. You have the knowledge, and we can show you how to share it.

In this book excerpt, you'll discover eight guiding principles—each brought to life by Mr. Carnegie's compelling, first-hand stories—designed to prepare you for powerful public speaking.

SPEAK MORE EFFECTIVELY
By Dale Carnegie

Part One
Public Speaking A Quick and Easy Way

You may be saying to yourself: "Is there really a quick and easy way to learn to speak in public—or is that merely an intriguing title that promises more than it delivers?"

No, I am not exaggerating. I am really going to let you in on a vital secret—a secret that will make it easier for you to speak in public immediately. Where did I discover this? In some book? No. In some college course on public speaking? No. I never even heard it mentioned there. I had to discover it the hard way—gradually, slowly, painfully.

If, back in my college days, someone had given me this password to effective speaking and writing, I could have saved myself years and years of wasted, heartbreaking effort. For example, I once wrote a book about Lincoln, and while writing it, I threw into the wastebasket at least a year of wasted effort that might have been saved had I known the great secrets that I am going to divulge to you.

The same thing happened when I spent two years trying to write a novel.

It happened again while writing a book on public speaking—another year of wasted effort thrown into the wastebasket because I didn't know the secrets of successful writing and speaking.

If Possible, Spend a Year in Preparation

What are these priceless secrets that I have been dangling before your eyes? Just this: talk about something that you have earned the right to talk about through long study or experience. Talk about something that you know and know that you know. Don't spend 10 minutes or 10 hours preparing a talk: spend 10 weeks or 10 months. Better still, spend 10 years.

Talk about something that has aroused your interest.

Talk about something that you have a deep desire to communicate to your listeners. To illustrate what I mean, let's take the case of Gay Kellogg, a housewife from Roselle, New Jersey. Gay Kellogg had never made a speech in public before she joined one of our classes in New York. She was terrified. She feared that public speaking might be an obscure art far beyond her abilities. Yet at the fourth session of the course, as she made an impromptu talk, she held the audience spellbound. I asked her to speak on "The Biggest Regret of My Life." Gay Kellogg then gave a talk that was deeply moving. The listeners could hardly keep the tears back. I know. I could hardly keep the tears from welling up in my own eyes. Her talk went like this:

"The biggest regret of my life is that I never knew a mother's love. My mother died when I was only a year old. I was brought up by a succession of aunts and other relatives who were so absorbed in their own children that they had no time for me. I never stayed with any of them very long. They were always sorry to see me come and glad to see me go.

"They never took any interest in me or gave me any affection. I knew I wasn't wanted. Even as a little child I could feel it. I often cried myself to sleep because of loneliness. The deepest desire of my heart was to have someone ask to see my report card from school. But no one ever did. No one cared. All I craved as a little child was love—and no one ever gave it to me."

Had Gay Kellogg spent ten years preparing that talk?

No. She had spent 20 years. She had been preparing herself to make that talk when she cried herself to sleep as a little child. She had been preparing herself to make that talk when her heart ached because no one asked to see her report card from school. No wonder she could talk about that subject. She could not have erased those early memories from her mind. Gay Kellogg had rediscovered a storehouse of tragic memories and feelings away deep down inside her. She didn't have to pump them up. She didn't have to work at making that talk. All she had to do was to let her pent-up feelings and memories rush up to the surface like oil from a well.

Jesus said: "My yoke is easy, my burden is light." So is the yoke and burden of good speaking. Ineffective talks are usually the ones that are written and memorized and sweated over and made artificial. Good talks are the ones that well up within you as a fountain. Many people talk the way I swim. I struggle and fight the water and wear myself out and go one-tenth as fast as the experts. Poor speakers, like poor swimmers, get taut and tense and twist themselves up into knots—and defeat their own purpose.

Become Excited About Your Subject

Even people with only mediocre speaking ability can give superb talks if they speak about something that has deeply stirred them. I saw a striking illustration of that years ago when I was conducting courses for the Brooklyn Chamber of Commerce. It was an example that I shall remember for a lifetime. It happened like this:

We were having a session devoted to impromptu talks. After the class assembled, I asked them to speak on "What, If Anything, Is Wrong with Religion?"

One member (a man, by the way, who had never finished high school) did something to that audience that I have never seen any other speaker do in the years I have been training people to speak in public. His talk was so moving that when he finished, every person in the room stood up in silent tribute.

This man told about the greatest tragedy of his life: the death of his mother. He was so devastated, so grief-stricken, that he no longer wanted to live. He said that when he went out of doors, even on a sunny day, it seemed as if he were wandering in a fog. He longed to die. In desperation, he went to his church and knelt and wept and said the rosary, and a great peace came over him—a divine peace of resignation: "Not my will, but Thine be done." As he finished his talk to the class, he said, in the voice of one who has had a revelation: "There is nothing wrong with religion! There is nothing wrong with God's love." I'll never forget that talk because of its emotional impact. When I congratulated the speaker on his deeply moving talk, he replied: "Yes, and I made it without any preparation."

Preparation? Well, if he hadn't prepared that talk, I don't know what preparation is. He meant, of course, that he had had no advance notice that he would have to talk on that subject. I am glad he didn't, because if he had had advance notice, his talk might have been far less effective. He might have labored over it and tried to make a speech and been artificial. Instead, he did just what Gay Kellogg did years later—he stood up and opened his heart and talked like one human being conversing with another.

The truth of the matter is that he was preparing to make that talk when he knelt and wept and said the rosary. Living, feeling, thinking, enduring "the slings and arrows of outrageous fortune"—that is the finest preparation ever yet devised for either speaking or writing.

Look Inside Yourself for Topics to Talk About

Do beginners know the necessity of looking inside themselves for topics? Know it? They never even heard of it! They are more likely to look inside a magazine for topics. For example, I remember meeting one of our students in the subway—a woman who was discouraged because she was making so little progress in this course. I asked her what she had talked about the previous week. I discovered that she had talked about whether Mussolini should be permitted to invade Ethiopia. She had gotten her information out of an article in Time Magazine. She had read the article twice. I asked her if she was interested in the subject, and she said, "No." I then asked her why she had talked about it. "Well," she replied. "I had to talk about something so I chose that."

Think of it: here was a woman who had tried to speak about Mussolini's Ethiopian war, yet she admitted she had little knowledge and no interest in the subject. She had neglected to speak on a subject she had earned the right to talk about.

After a discussion, I said to her: "I would listen with respect and interest if you spoke about something you have experienced and know about, but neither I nor anyone else would be interested in a subject which you yourself are not interested in, such as Mussolini's invasion of Ethiopia. You don't know enough about it to merit our attention or respect."

Talk From Your Heart—Not From a Book

Many students of public speaking are like that woman. They want to get their subjects out of a book or a magazine instead of from their own knowledge and convictions. For example, a few years ago, I was one of the three judges in an intercollegiate speaking contest over the NBC network. The judges never saw the speakers. We listened to them from Studio 8G in Radio City. I wish, oh, how I wish that every student and teacher of public speaking could have witnessed what went on in that studio. The first speaker spoke on "Democracy at the Crossroads."

The next one spoke about "How to Prevent War." It was painfully evident that they were merely repeating carefully rehearsed and memorized words. So neither the guest in the studio nor the judges paid much attention to them. One of the judges was Willem Hendrik Van Loon. When he began drawing a cartoon of one of the contestants, everyone stood and watched him and ignored the amateurish "orations," the memorized words, which were coming over the air.

However, the next speaker caught my attention immediately. A senior at Yale, he spoke about what was wrong with the colleges. He had earned the right to talk about that. We listened to him with respect. But the speaker who got the first prize began something like this:

"I have just come from a hospital where a friend of mine is near death because of an automobile accident. Most automobile accidents are caused by the younger generation. I am a member of that generation and I want to speak to you about the causes of these accidents."

Everyone in the studio was quiet as he spoke. He was talking about realities, not trying to make a speech. He was speaking about something that he had earned the right to talk about. He was talking from the inside out.

Have an Eager Desire to Communicate

However, let me warn you that merely earning the right to talk about a subject will not always produce a superb talk. Another element must be added—an element that is vital in speaking. Briefly, it is this: in addition to earning the right to speak, we must have a deep and abiding desire to communicate our convictions and transfer our feelings to our listeners.

To illustrate: suppose I were asked to talk about raising corn and hogs. I spent twenty years on a corn and hog farm in Missouri, so surely I have earned the right to talk on that subject. I don't have any special desire to talk on that subject. But suppose I were asked to speak on what was wrong with the kind of education I got in college. I could hardly fail if I talked on that subject, because I would have the three basic requirements for a good talk. First, I would be talking about something that I had earned the right to talk about. Second, I would have deep feelings and convictions that I longed to convey to you. Third, I would have clear and convincing illustrations out of my own experience.

When Gay Kellogg spoke on the biggest regret of her life—never knowing a mother's love—she had not only earned the right through suffering to talk on that subject, but she also had a deep emotional desire to tell us about it. So did the class member who spoke in the Brooklyn Chamber of Commerce class about the death of his mother—"Not my will, but Thine be done."

History has repeatedly been changed by people who had the desire and the ability to transfer their convictions and emotions to their listeners. If John Wesley had not had that desire and ability, he could never have founded a religious sect that has girdled the globe. If Peter the Hermit had not had that desire and ability, he could never have stirred the imagination of the world and plunged Europe into the futile and bloody Crusades for possession of the Holy Land. If Hitler had not had the innate ability to transfer his hate and bitterness to his listeners, he could not have seized power in Germany and plunged the world into war.

Talk About Your Experiences

You are prepared right now to make at least a dozen good talks—talks that no one else on earth could make except you, because no one else has ever had precisely the same experience that you have had. What are these subjects? I don't know. But you do. So carry a sheet of paper with you for a few weeks and write down, as you think of them, all the subjects that you are prepared to talk about through experience—subjects such as "The Biggest Regret of My Life," "My Biggest Ambition," and "Why I Liked (Disliked) School." Do that and you will be surprised how quickly your list of topics will grow.

Here is good news for you: your progress as a speaker will depend far more on your choosing the right topic to talk about than upon your native ability as a speaker. You can feel at ease and make a fine talk immediately if you will only do what Gay Kellogg did: talk about some experience that has affected you deeply, some experience you have been thinking about for twenty years. But you may never feel completely at ease if you try to make speeches about "Mussolini's Invasion of Ethiopia" or "Democracy at the Crossroads."

Talk About Things You Have Studied

Talking about your own experiences is obviously the quickest way to develop courage and self-confidence. But after you have gained a bit of experience, you will want to talk about other subjects. What subjects? And where can you find them? Everywhere. For example, I once asked a class of executives of the New York Telephone Company to jot down every idea for a speech that occurred to them during the week. It was November. One person saw Thanksgiving Day printed in red on the calendar and spoke about the many things for which to be thankful. Another person saw some pigeons on the street. That inspired an idea. The person gave a talk about pigeons that I shall never forget. But the prize winner that night was a class member who had seen a bedbug crawling up a man's collar in the subway. The class member gave us a talk that I still remember after twenty years.

Carry a Scribbling Book

Why don't you do what Voltaire did? Voltaire, one of the most powerful writers of the eighteenth century, carried in his pocket what he called a "scribbling book"—a book in which he jotted down his fleeting thoughts and ideas. Why don't you carry a "scribbling book?" Then, if you are irritated by a discourteous clerk, for example, jot down the word "Discourtesy" in your scribbling book.

Then try to recall two or three other striking incidents of discourtesy. Select the best one and tell us what we ought to do about it. Presto! You have a two-minute talk on Discourtesy.

As soon as you begin to look for topics for talks, you will find them everywhere: in the home, the office, the street.

Say Something Simple

Don't attempt to speak on some world-shaking problem such as "The Atomic Bomb." Take something simple— almost anything will do, provided the idea gets you, instead of your getting the idea. For example, I recently heard a student of this course, Mary A. Leer, of Chicago, talk on "Back Doors." You may find her talk dull as you read it; but if you had only listened to it, as I did, you would have loved it because she herself was positively excited about her back door. In fact, I never before heard anyone speak with such glowing enthusiasm about painting the back door! The point I am trying to make is this: almost any subject will do for a talk provided you yourself have earned the right to talk about it through study or experience, and are excited about it and eager to tell us about it.

This Is the Famous Talk About Back Doors!

"Four years ago, when I moved into my present apartment, the back door was painted a drab shade of gray. It was terrible. Every time I opened the back door it gave me a depressed feeling. So I bought a can of beautiful blue paint and painted the outside of the back door, the jambs and the inside of the screen door. That paint was the most exquisite shade of blue that I had ever seen; and every time I opened the back door after that, it seemed as though I was looking upon a bit of heaven.

"I was never more angry in my life than when I came home one evening not long ago and found that the house painter had pried open my screen door and painted my beautiful blue door a most hideous shade of putty gray. I could have cheerfully choked that painter.

"You can tell a lot more about people from their back doors than you can from their front doors. Front doors are often prettied up just to impress you. But back doors tell tales. A slovenly back door tattles on slovenly housekeeping. But a back door that is painted a cheerful color and has pots of blooming plants sitting around and garbage cans that are painted and orderly, that kind of back door tells you that there is an interesting person with a lively imagination living behind it. I have already bought a can of beautiful blue paint; and next Saturday, I am going to have a gorgeous time. I am again going to make my back door cheerful and inspiring."

And so it goes. A volume could be filled with examples to show the power of speakers who:

1. Have earned the right, by study and experience, to talk about their subject;
2. Are excited about it themselves; and
3. Are eager to communicate their ideas and feelings to their listeners.

How to Prepare and Deliver Your Talks

Here are 8 principles that will help immensely in preparing your talks:

I. Make brief notes of the interesting things you want to mention.

II. Don't write out your talks.

Why? Because if you do, you will use written language instead of easy, conversational language; and when you stand up to talk, you will probably find yourself trying to remember what you wrote. That will keep you from speaking naturally and with sparkle.

III. Never, never, never memorize a talk word for word.

If you memorize your talk, you are almost sure to forget it; and the audience will probably be glad, for nobody wants to listen to a canned speech. Even if you don't forget it, it will sound memorized. You will have a faraway look in your eyes and a faraway ring in your voice. You won't sound like a human being trying to tell us something.

If, in a longer talk, you are afraid you will forget what you want to say, then make some brief notes and hold them in your hand and glance at them occasionally. That is what I usually do.

IV. Fill your talk with illustrations and examples.

By far the easiest way to make a talk interesting is to fill it with examples. To illustrate what I mean, let's take this booklet you are reading now. Approximately half of those pages are devoted to illustration. First, there is the illustration of Gay Kellogg's talk about the suffering she endured as a child. Next, the illustration of the speaker on "What, If Anything, Is Wrong with Religion?" Next, the example of the woman who tried to talk on Mussolini's invasion of Ethiopia. That is followed by the story of the four college students in a speaking contest over the radio—and so on. My biggest problem in writing a book or preparing a speech is not to get ideas, but to get illustrations to make those ideas clear, vivid, and unforgettable. The old Roman philosophers used to say, "Exemplum docet" (the example teaches). And how right they were!

For example, let me show you the value of an illustration. Years ago, a congressman made a stormy speech accusing the government of wasting our money by printing useless pamphlets. He illustrated what he meant by saying the government had printed a pamphlet on "The Love Life of the Bullfrog." I would have forgotten that speech years ago if it hadn't been for that one specific illustration, "The Love Life of the Bullfrog." I may forget a million other facts as the decades pass, but I'll never forget his charge that the government wastes our money by printing and giving away pamphlets such as "The Love Life of the Bullfrog!"

Exemplum docet. Not only does the example teach, but it is about the only thing that does teach. I have heard brilliant speeches which I promptly forgot because there were no examples to make them stick in my memory.

V. Know far more about your subject than you can use.

Ida Tarbell, one of America's most distinguished writers, told me that years ago, while in London, she received a cable from S.S. McClure, the founder of McClure's Magazine, asking her to write a two-page article on the Atlantic Cable. Miss Tarbell interviewed the London manager of the Atlantic Cable and got all the information necessary to write her five-hundred word article. But she didn't stop there. She went to the British Museum library and read magazine articles and books about the Atlantic Cable, and the biography of Cyrus West Field, the man who laid the Atlantic Cable. She studied cross sections of cables on display in the British Museum, and then visited a factory on the outskirts of London and saw cables being manufactured. "When I finally wrote those two typewritten pages on the Atlantic Cable," Miss Tarbell said, as she told me the story, "I had enough material to write a small book about it. But that vast amount of material which I had and did not use enabled me to write what I did write with confidence and clarity and interest. It gave me reserve power."

Ida Tarbell had learned through years of experience that she had to earn the right to write over five hundred words about the Atlantic Cable. The same principle goes for speaking. Make yourself something of an authority on your subject. Develop that priceless asset known as reserve power.

VI. Rehearse your talk by conversing with your friends.

Will Rogers prepared his famous Sunday night radio talks by trying them out as conversation on the people he met during the week. If, for example, he wanted to speak on the gold standard, he would wisecrack about it in conversation during the week. He would then discover which of his jokes went over, which remarks elicited people's interest. That is an infinitely better way to rehearse a talk than to try it out with gestures in front of a mirror.

VII. Instead of worrying about your delivery, find ways of improving it.

Much harmful, misleading nonsense has been written about delivery of a speech. The truth is that when you face an audience, you should forget all about voice, breathing, gestures, posture, emphasis. Forget everything except what you are saying. What listeners want, as Hamlet's mother said, is "more matter, with less art." Do what a cat does when trying to catch a mouse. It doesn't look around and say: "I wonder how my tail looks, and I wonder if I am standing right, and how is my facial expression?" Oh, no. That cat is so intent on catching a mouse for dinner that it couldn't stand wrong or look wrong if it tried—and neither can you if you are so vitally interested in your audience and in what you are saying that you forget yourself.

Don't imagine that expressing your ideas and emotions before an audience is something that requires years of technical training like you have to devote to mastering music or painting. Anybody can make a splendid talk at home when angry. For example, if somebody hauled off and knocked you down this instant, you would get up and make a superb talk. Your gestures, your posture, your facial expression would be perfect because they would be the expressions of genuine anger. And remember, you don't have to learn to express your emotions. You could express your emotions superbly when you were six months old. Ask any mother.

Watch a group of children at play. What fine expression! What perfect emphasis, gestures, posture, communication! Jesus said: "Except ye become as little children, ye cannot enter the kingdom of heaven." Yes, and unless you become as natural and spontaneous and free as little children at play, you cannot enter the realm of good expression.

VIII. Don't imitate others; be yourself.

I first came to New York to study at the American Academy of Dramatic Arts. I aspired to be an actor. I had what I thought was a brilliant idea, a shortcut to success. My campaign to achieve excellence was so simple, so foolproof, that I was unable to comprehend why thousands of ambitious people hadn't already discovered it. It was this: I would study the famous actors of that day—John Drew, E. H. Sothern, Walter Hampden and Otis Skinner. Then I would imitate the best points of each one of them and make myself into a shining, triumphant combination of all of them. How silly! How tragic! I had to waste years of my life imitating other people before it penetrated my thick

Missouri skull that I had to be myself, and that I couldn't possibly be anyone else.

To illustrate what I mean: A number of years ago, I set out to write the best book on public speaking for business people that had ever been written. I had the same foolish idea about writing this book that I had formerly had about acting: I was going to borrow the ideas of many other writers and put them all in one book—a book that would have everything. So I got scores of books on public speaking and spent a year incorporating their ideas in my manuscript. But it finally dawned on me once again that I was playing the fool.

This hodgepodge of other people's ideas that I had written was so synthetic, so dull that no business person would ever stumble through it. So I tossed a year's work into the wastebasket, and started all over again. This time I said to myself: "You've got to be Dale Carnegie, with all his faults and limitations. You can't possibly be anybody else." So I quit trying to be a combination of other people, and rolled up my sleeves and did what I should have done in the first place: I wrote a textbook on public speaking out of my own experiences, observations and convictions.

Why don't you profit from my stupid waste of time? Don't try to imitate others.

How are you preparing for that big talk or presentation you have coming up? Understand more about how to engage, persuade and inspirc audiences in Dale Carnegie's High Impact Presentations program. Learn more at dalecarnegie.com.

INDEX